• HALSGROVE DISCOVER SERIES ➤

WILD HAMPSHIRE & ISLE OF WIGHT

Written by Clive Chatters
Picture editing by Abi Jarvis

HALSGROVE

Title page: Dormouse © Eliana Sevianu

First published in Great Britain in 2010.

Copyright © Hampshire & Isle of Wight Wildlife Trust 2010.

All rights reserved. No part of this publication may be reproduced,
stored in a retrieval system, or transmitted in any form or by any
means without the prior permission of the copyright holder.

British Library Cataloguing-in-Publication Data
A CIP record for this title is available from the British Library

ISBN 978 1 84114 856 4

HALSGROVE
Halsgrove House,
Ryelands Industrial Estate,
Bagley Road, Wellington, Somerset TA21 9PZ
Tel: 01823 653777   Fax: 01823 216796
email: sales@halsgrove.com

Part of the Halsgrove group of companies
Information on all Halsgrove titles is available at: www.halsgrove.com

Printed and bound by Grafiche Flaminia, Italy

ACKNOWLEDGEMENTS

THE TRUST WISHES TO THANK the following people for their kindness in supplying information for the book, whether they were aware of doing so or not: Michael Bryant, Graham Darrah, Jean and Richard Hedley, Bob Page, Jenni Tubbs, Jim White and Eddie Wiseman together with Trust staff, past and present.

The production of this book was greatly assisted by the contributions of many photographers, all of whom have been credited alongside their images. The Trust would like to give special thanks to its team of volunteer photographers, and to the following organisations, individuals and websites in supplying their images:

Alex MacNaughton, Andy Browne, Bill Truckle, chalto.co.uk, Damian Waters (drumimages.co.uk), Darin Smith, Dave Foker, David Kilbey, Dennis Bright, flickr.com, floralimages.co.uk, Hampshire County Council, Ian Pratt, Ian Ralphs, Imperial War Museum, Jason Crook, Ken Dolbear, Ladybird Books Ltd, Matt Doggett, Mike Read, New Forest National Park Authority, Paul Naylor (marinephoto.co.uk), Pelican Graphics, Peter Durnell, Portsmouth City Council, Simon Booth, South Downs Joint Committee, the Barker-Mill Estate, *The News* (Portsmouth), Tony Bates, Tony Wootton, ukwildflowers.com, Winchester City Council.

And finally, the Hampshire & Isle of Wight Wildlife Trust editorial team: Debbie Tann, Lisa Chilton, Sally Hayns, Abi Jarvis (Picture Editor), Sarah Hayward and Jason Crook.

Hampshire & Isle of Wight Wildlife Trust, Beechcroft House, Vicarage Lane, Curdridge, Hants SO32 2DP.
Tel: 01489 774400. Email: feedback@hwt.org.uk Web: www.hwt.org.uk
Registered Charity No: 201081. Company Limited by guarantee & registered in England No. 676313.

Bee orchid.
© Mark Heighes

CONTENTS

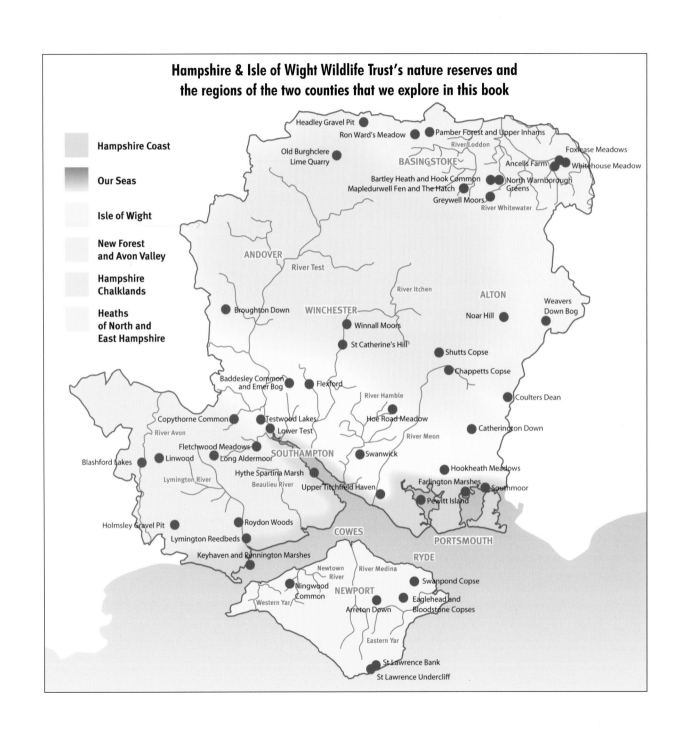

Hampshire & Isle of Wight Wildlife Trust's nature reserves and the regions of the two counties that we explore in this book

Hampshire Coast

Our Seas

Isle of Wight

New Forest and Avon Valley

Hampshire Chalklands

Heaths of North and East Hampshire

Headley Gravel Pit
Ron Ward's Meadow
Pamber Forest and Upper Inhams
River Loddon
BASINGSTOKE
Old Burghclere Lime Quarry
Foxlease Meadows
Ancells Farm
Whitehouse Meadow
Bartley Heath and Hook Common
North Warnborough Greens
Mapledurwell Fen and The Hatch
Greywell Moors
River Whitewater
ANDOVER
River Test
River Itchen
ALTON
Weavers Down Bog
Broughton Down
WINCHESTER
Noar Hill
Winnall Moors
St Catherine's Hill
Shutts Copse
Chappetts Copse
Baddesley Common and Emer Bog
Flexford
River Hamble
Coulters Dean
Copythorne Common
Testwood Lakes
Hoe Road Meadow
Catherington Down
River Avon
Lower Test
River Meon
Fletchwood Meadows
Long Aldermoor
SOUTHAMPTON
Swanwick
Blashford Lakes
Linwood
Hythe Spartina Marsh
Hookheath Meadows
Lymington River
Beaulieu River
Upper Titchfield Haven
Farlington Marshes
Southmoor
Pewitt Island
Holmsley Gravel Pit
Roydon Woods
COWES
PORTSMOUTH
Lymington Reedbeds
RYDE
Keyhaven and Pennington Marshes
Newtown River
River Medina
Swanpond Copse
Ningwood Common
NEWPORT
Eaglehead and Bloodstone Copses
Western Yar
Arreton Down
Eastern Yar
St Lawrence Bank
St Lawrence Undercliff

FOREWORD

THE SHEER BRILLIANCE of beech woodland when the buds burst in May. The intensity of purple heather when the heaths blush in August. The sparkling clarity of a cold winter sky filled with wheeling geese. The subdued richness of a misty October beneath the ancient oaks, where fungi glow, deer tread silently and early owls hoot. The simple secrecy of a wasteland den where fox cubs wrestle, their yaps drowned by the din of traffic. All are Hampshire regulars. The county's natural diversity is possibly unsurpassed in the UK, and when you add the unspoiled habitats of the Isle of Wight you have an internationally important assemblage of wildlife. Some of these sights are almost unique, notably our chalk streams and sandy lowland heaths. And importantly, most of these places are accessible to us all, in the counties' fantastic collection of nature reserves and other protected areas.

© Paul Greenan

Such is the abundance of species in our two counties. We have the rare, the glamorous, the bizarre and the beautiful. The author's admiration, lifelong experience and enthusiasm for the region shine through in this great exploration of our local life. The result is a treat, with text and pictures to tempt you out to discover it all for yourself. You will be astonished to learn that so much is on your doorstep. So stop dreaming of distant safaris, don't let familiarity breed contempt, and use this book as the inspiration to experience your own face to face encounters with an amazing flora and fauna.

In 2011, Hampshire & Isle of Wight Wildlife Trust celebrates its 50th anniversary and it's a well deserved landmark. The charity has established a legacy of great nature reserves, as well as huge amounts of data to influence local conservation policy and practice. But for all this, and all the wonderful life that the areas contain, the contemporary pressures on our part of southern England are massive. There is no room for complacency – we need your help. So please, read, enjoy, explore and then help conserve this remarkable part of the world.

Chris Packham
New Forest, 2010.

Arreton Down nature reserve,
Isle of Wight. © Chris Archbold

INTRODUCTION

THIS BOOK HAS BEEN written to mark the 50th anniversary of the founding of Hampshire & Isle of Wight Wildlife Trust. It is a celebration of the wealth of wildlife in our two counties and why we must continue our efforts to protect and enhance it in the years to come.

We have not sought to provide an audit of our wildlife heritage. Many wonderful species and nature reserves do not get a mention for reasons of space rather than significance. Similarly this is not an official history of the Trust. What this book offers is a journey around the two counties exploring the breadth of habitats and species, as well as the Trust's work to protect them.

In researching the book, a number of strong themes came shining through. The foresight of the founders of the Trust was remarkable. Ideas about nature conservation that were expressed some 50 years ago are still fresh and relevant today. These include the recognition that nature reserves alone, if managed in isolation from their surrounding environment, cannot secure a long-term future for our threatened habitats and species. Instead we must strive to integrate protected areas into the wider landscape and the economy, working with landowners, businesses and local communities. The Trust's founders recognised the importance of working with others, and understood the many benefits of partnerships, as well as the simple fact that the job is too big for us to tackle alone. Another ideal that has had an enduring impact on the Trust's work is the need to inspire, engage and educate others – especially young people – so that they may support and champion nature conservation into the future.

There are, naturally, many stories drawn from the Trust's archives or from first-hand accounts of the people who have known the Trust from its early years. A selection of these has been used to tell the story of the Trust and of progress in nature conservation over the past five decades. Writing a book that is, in part, historical is fraught in deciding who may be mentioned. There are so many people who have given so much to the Trust, some in the public eye, others quietly working in the background. It is not possible to include them all. A mention here is not meant to place any role or contribution above that of others.

Above all, it is hoped that in reading this book you will be inspired by the richness of our counties' wildlife, and by those whose commitment and vision have helped to safeguard it over the last 50 years. Most importantly, it is hoped that you will support the Trust as it faces the challenges of protecting wildlife into the future.

Pearl-bordered fritillary on bugle. The caterpillars of this rare butterfly feed on violets growing in woodland clearings and are often associated with hazel coppice.
© Graham Hoggarth

The chaffinch is a familiar sight in gardens, woodlands, hedgerows and fields. Its neat little nests, made out of grass and leaves, are hidden by moss and lichen. Feeding on insects and seeds, and with a loud call, it is the most colourful and well known of our finches.
© Dave Foker

13

The chalk rivers of Hampshire rise from the downs, flowing either north into the Thames or south into the Solent's estuaries. Chalk rivers exhibit clear water and constant flow from their groundwater-fed springs. Beds of starwort and water crowfoot grow over the clean gravel beds to provide cover for a great diversity of fish including salmon, brown trout, lamprey and bullhead. © Dennis Bright

IN THE GRAND SCHEME OF THINGS

THE TWO COUNTIES OF Hampshire and the Isle of Wight might not immediately spring to mind as world-class wildlife hotspots – but that is exactly what they are. Just why we are so blessed with this abundance of wildlife and wild places is the result of a number of factors. Compared with much of the Continent, the British Isles are warm and wet, providing comfortable living conditions for a wide range of wildlife. Our two counties, sitting in the centre of England's south coast, benefit from an especially moderate climate, sandwiched between cooler, drier climes to the east and warmer, wetter climes to the south and west. As a result, our land, seas and skies are home to a unique mix of wildlife: the best of both worlds. The extreme southern coast of the Isle of Wight even boasts species more usually associated with the Mediterranean.

Adding to the diversity is the extraordinarily varied geology of Hampshire and the Isle of Wight, giving us a spectacular array of landscapes, from downlands, heaths, cliffs and sea caves, to great rivers, floodplains, mudflats and shingle spits. Each of these landscapes attracts a different community of wildlife.

The red cage fungus is a species of central and southern Europe, which also grows in Hampshire and on the Island due to the warm climate here. The species is gradually becoming more widespread in southern England.
© Dave Gough

Of all the wildlife treasures of our two counties, several stand out as truly world-class. One is the great flocks of water birds, tens of thousands strong, which pass the winter on our muddy shores. Most of these birds breed in the frozen lands of Siberia and the Arctic, before heading south to take advantage of our milder winters and the phenomenal abundance of food to be found here. Indeed, the two counties' shores are a critical stopping-off point on the East Atlantic Flyway, one of the world's great bird migration routes linking the Arctic regions to southern Africa.

Another unmissable highlight is the New Forest, now a National Park. The Forest's extensive heathlands with their abundant wildlife were shaped first by herds of wild oxen and deer, and latterly, over many centuries, by domestic animals including ponies, cattle and pigs. Other landscapes, from the majestic South Downs to the coppiced woodlands of the Isle of Wight, also owe their special character to the influence of historic land-use.

More special places in the two counties, from beautiful chalk rivers, cliffs and sea caves to estuaries, lagoons and wildflower-rich shingle beaches, are outstanding examples of habitats that, on a global scale, are exceptionally rare. We are privileged to have them.

This combination of features, together with the wildlife and wild places described in later pages, mark out Hampshire and the Island as a truly outstanding area, offering more than a lifetime's worth of discovery and enjoyment for all.

Opposite: The Solent coast is part of a worldwide chain of wetlands which support migrating flocks of birds, such as these brent geese. Many birds, particularly some species of wading bird, use these wetlands as stepping stones for greater journeys to Africa and beyond.
© Tony Bates, chalto.co.uk

The British Isles hold the greatest population of bluebells on Earth due to the oceanic climate. Each spring our ancient woodlands mount a spectacular display of what, for us, are common wildflowers.
© Linda Priestley

THE TRUST'S EARLY YEARS

IN MAY 1960, EDWIN COHEN, a leading Hampshire ornithologist, travelled to Skegness to join fellow naturalists on the wild headland of Gibraltar Point. The meeting had been called to discuss the formation of county-based Naturalists' Trusts. At that time this was a novel idea. Whilst Nathaniel Rothschild and the Society for the Promotion of Nature Reserves had advocated this approach as far back as 1912, in the spring of 1960 there were only eight such Trusts in existence. By the time the group met again in September that year, plans for the Trust for Hampshire and the Isle of Wight were well advanced.

At this time, the country was emerging from the trauma and austerity of the Second World War into the confidence and economic dynamism of the 1960s. The war years were remarkable as a time not only when the nation fought for its very survival, but also when deep thought was given to what we were fighting for. The immediate post-war years saw the fulfilment of that thinking, with the establishment of modern Britain. The nation's commitment to agriculture, our local government system, the National Health Service and social security all arose from this period. The conservation and enjoyment of what was important about our wildlife and wild spaces was also an important part of this movement. Through the war years, government committees set out the framework for much of our current system of protection for landscapes and wildlife. Landscape protection was incorporated into the National Parks and Access to the Countryside Act of 1949, and nature conservation was progressed by the new statutory agency, the Nature Conservancy, established by Royal Charter in the same year.

Opposite, top: Stanley Street in Portsmouth following the blitz of the city in late summer 1940.
© The News, Portsmouth

Opposite, bottom: The meeting of county naturalists at Gibraltar Point in May 1960.
© Permission of Lincolnshire Wildlife Trust

The Dartford warbler was adopted by the newly-founded Trust as its emblem. The harsh winter of 1963 reduced what was already a rare bird to a national population of just 11 pairs. The birds gradually recovered and, with a succession of mild winters, the population has recently grown to over 3,000 pairs. Hampshire's heathlands remain a national stronghold for this insect-eating bird of tall heather and dense gorse.
© David Whistlecraft

The responsibility for caring for wild nature was not seen to rest wholly with government. Local people were combining their energies to establish local charities such as the Trust. The Hampshire & Isle of Wight Naturalists Trust became fully incorporated as a company on the 28th November 1960 and was registered as a charity in the following year. The eight founding members were an architect, a medical research assistant, three university lecturers, a retired Army officer, a bank manager and a solicitor.

Remarkably, the minutes of the founding meetings illustrate issues and approaches that are all too familiar today. The most important places for wildlife in the counties were being identified; representations were being made to protect them from harmful development and initiatives taken to secure them in safe hands. As early as 14th January 1961 a sub-committee of Trust was established to *consider the modifications made by the Minister to proposals for the Hampshire Greenbelt, and produce evidence for objections…*". At the same time the Trust sought to establish nature reserves, noting that *"While it is most desirable to conserve large areas, small spaces must also be considered if the biological interest is sufficient"*.

For over 50 years the Trust has enjoyed great continuity in its work. Michael Bryant (far left) was a founder member of the Trust. Here he is joined by Trust staff (left to right) Bob Page (1976-1999), Clive Chatters (1989-present) and Jim White, the Trust's first paid conservation officer (1973-76). © Alan Inder

The Trust was also quick to establish close links with local authority planning officers. From the early years, the Trust was participating in the planning process, including giving evidence at public inquiries. At the time, a new plan for major urban growth in Hampshire was being prepared, and the Trust challenged threats to Silchester and Bordon from proposed new towns and to Calshot from a power station.

The Trust's early thinking came together in an internal paper, produced in the mid 1960s. With regard to the impact on wildlife of accelerating urban growth, the paper advised: *"We cannot keep back the economic tide but it should be one of the prime duties of the Trust to become aware of these potential developments and to make developers aware of conservation needs"*. The Trust achieved this through the use of science and quiet diplomacy, as well as a willingness to pursue the cause all the way to public inquiry.

The importance of educating future generations in understanding the environment was reflected in the recommendation that *"the Trust should secure a well distributed series of reserves which would be used primarily for educational purposes…"*. In 1962 a Trust committee member was given the role of Education Secretary, promoting wildlife as a resource for both 'learning and doing'. Wildlife offered opportunities to teach natural sciences but was also a means to direct youthful energy to practical tasks.

The establishment of nature reserves was a key part of the Trust's work. Nature reserves were seen to serve many purposes. These included the safeguarding of sites at risk and the protection both of rare species and of those species that need *"space or seclusion to be viable"*. It was recommended that there be a good spread of reserves, both geographically and covering a range of habitats.

The advice included the prophetic statement: *"Preservation of Places of Interest... is not sufficient alone. There is a need to ensure that our reserves are not left like islands in a sea of suburban development, since they would soon lose their Natural History interest under such conditions"*.

It was not the intention of the Trust to seek to include all wildlife-rich land within nature reserves. The role of private and public landowners in caring for their own land was recognised and respected, with the Trust offering support and advice.

These themes of participation in the planning world, investment in education and public enjoyment, establishing nature reserves and working with landowners permeate the first 50 years of the Trust's work, and remain the cornerstone of the Trust's approach today and into the future.

Following the Trust's change of name from 'Naturalists Trust' to 'Wildlife Trust' in 1991, the Trust logo has changed several times. Replacing the Dartford warbler with the badger was a symbol of the Trust's commitment to the national partnership of The Wildlife Trusts.

Opposite: Modern Portsmouth is the backdrop for the vast flocks of dark-bellied brent geese that gather every winter in the Solent Harbours.
© Steve Page

The mudflats of the Hampshire coast are a rich feeding ground. Exposed at low tide, they are a vital resource for coastal wading birds and wildfowl. When the flats are submerged at high tide, fish, shrimps and crabs move in for their share of the feast. © Mark Heighes

THE HAMPSHIRE COAST

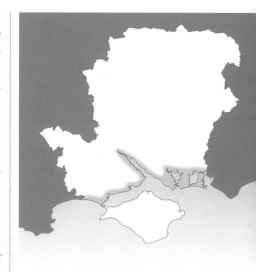

THE LANDSCAPE OF THE English coast has never stood still, and our two counties' coastlines are no exception.   At the end of the last ice age, the chalk cliffs stretching from Purbeck to West Wight were breached to form the Solent. Since then our coastline has been slowly migrating inland. Where there are hard rocks, this process creates high cliffs. Along the softer coasts of the Solent Harbours and Southampton Water these forces are equally powerful but less dramatic.

Every tide, twice a day, day in and day out, the sea presses against the land. The high tides run up the river valleys and across the platforms of the saltmarshes. Historic low-lying plains that were the homes of our ancestors are now the tidal basins of our harbours. Everything that lives on the coast needs to adapt to these changes.

Much of Hampshire's coast has been modified by urban growth, and across large areas the tides are held back by sea walls. Each successive generation needs bigger and better sea walls to safeguard the prosperity of our coastal cities. Amongst this urbanity is one of the least modified stretches of our coast: at the head of Southampton Water are the marshes of the Lower Test.

Portsmouth Harbour is now almost completely surrounded by urban areas including the Royal Naval dockyards. The loss of farmland adjacent to the mudflats and marshes has reduced the area available to support overwintering birds. At high tide, birds have to consume precious energy to find somewhere to roost or feed above the level of the flood. © Jason Crook

25

Coastal grazing marshes support a wide range of species.

Top: The cattle on coastal marshes are troubled by some of Britain's largest biting flies. This female biting fly (*Haematopota pluvialis*) feeds on the blood of any mammal it can find. The saliva of this group of biting flies is now being studied by scientists investigating the treatment of people suffering from blood-clots and problems with blood pressure.
© Ray Wilson Photography

Bottom left: In early summer the tall reed-fringes along ungrazed watercourses are filled with the chattering song of the sedge warbler, newly arrived from Africa.
© John Windust

Bottom right: Freshwater often flows into grazing marshes, either through rivers or by way of discrete springs. Here wildflowers of fens and riverine marshes can be found, such as the water avens.
© www.ukwildflowers.com

Lower Test Marshes and Testwood Lakes nature reserves

The Lower Test Marshes are a part of the Barker-Mill Estate, one of the great landed estates of Hampshire. In the mid 1970s, Trust voluntary wardens worked with the Estate to oversee the marshes. At first this was a lively task, with accounts of gangs of armed poachers pursuing wardens through the reedbeds. Over the decades, the Trust gradually took on additional responsibilities, including the grazing and overall management of the marshes. The original nature reserve has been added to over the years by acquiring leases from neighbours and making small freehold purchases. It now extends to some 150 hectares. In the late 1990s, Southern Water developed Testwood Lakes as part of the water supply for South Hampshire. This opportunity enabled the Trust to establish an education centre together with a further 60 hectares of nature reserve. The Testwood Lakes centre opened in 2003 and now provides facilities to welcome visitors to the Lower Test Valley.

The Lower Test is a place of great diversity. The short salty turf of the southern marshes is ideal grazing for wintering flocks of teal and wigeon. The slightly fresher reedbeds provide roosts for congregations of swallow, as well as a vital feeding ground to prime them before migration. In the waters where the salt and fresh water mix, migratory fish such as sea trout and salmon adjust to the radically different environment before continuing upstream to breed. Far more flexible in their movements between the land and sea are the otters that re-colonised the Test in the 1990s. The Lower Test is a crossroads of land and sea, a meeting of the urban and the natural.

The marsh marigold is the herald of spring in the marshes of the Lower Test. This is the largest British member of the buttercup family. Whereas marsh marigold needs freshwater, the closely related hairy buttercup and celery-leaved buttercup grow in brackish soils where saltwater floods the marsh at high tide.
© www.ukwildflowers.com

For centuries Redbridge (once known as Reedbridge) has been a safe crossing of the river and the marshes. Bundled into this narrow corridor are the trunk road and the mainline railway. Here the salt of the estuary mixes with the freshwater of the River Test. This is an extraordinary landscape, a picture of high-rise homes, striding pylons and the roar of traffic, mixed with cattle wandering through reedy marshes, peacefully chewing the cud amongst great flocks of estuary birds.

In recent years there has been growing concern about climate change. As the world warms, water is released into the seas from melting ice. The resulting increase in sea level is exacerbated due to warm water taking up more space than cold water. To add to these changes, the southern coast of England is still settling down after the last ice age. Slowly but surely, the land is sinking. The combined effect is for the sea to rise, in relation to the land, by about six millimetres a year. At first this may seem a small matter, less than the thickness of a pencil. Yet year on year the millimetres add up. Over the course of a lifetime what would have been dry ground to a baby would be knee deep water to the newly retired.

In recent years, the migration of saltwater upstream has led to willow trees dying off and being replaced by brackish marshland. The wild dynamism of the Lower Test Marshes is in stark contrast to the tower blocks and dockyard cranes of neighbouring Southampton. © Clive Chatters

As the tide rises and falls, dabbling ducks can be seen feeding at the water's edge. Teal feed mostly on seeds, picking them off individual plants or filtering the water or mud.
© Damian Waters, drumimages.co.uk

Boardwalks and stepping stones guide the cautious walker through the marshes. At high tides the whole area can be flooded so that only the very tops of the tallest reeds are showing. The animals of the marsh move to higher ground or perch high in the reeds. © Mark Heighes

The Lower Test Marshes is one of very few places along the coast of our two counties where this change is happening naturally, unfettered by built obstacles that would restrict the movement of the habitats and wildlife. Measurement and observation of the changes here provide an intriguing insight into the impacts of climate change. Between 1996 and 2003, the upper limit of the saltmarshes shifted more than 150 metres inland. While the speed of movement appeared to slow between 2003 and 2008, those areas with some salt influence have become even saltier. Within the freshwater reaches of the marsh, where the rising tide meets the flowing river, the higher tides now hold back the seaward flow of the freshwater river for longer. The land no longer drains in the way it once did. What, until recently, were hay meadows, are now becoming marshland.

At the Lower Test Marshes it is fortunate that there is space for nature to flex and adapt to the changing environment. Unfortunately such opportunities for nature to accommodate change are the exception rather than the rule.

Farlington Marshes nature reserve

Towards the eastern end of the Solent are the great expanses of intertidal muds and marshes of Chichester and Langstone Harbours. In the late eighteenth century, at the time of the building of Nelson's navy, a sea wall was built around some of the marshes of the Manor of Farlington. Early maps show us how today's Farlington Marshes were once a small part of a very much larger complex of marsh and ooze that lined the margins of Langstone Harbour. This great landscape, with its many coastal farms and manors, has now gone; the last survivor is the Trust's nature reserve, Farlington Marshes.

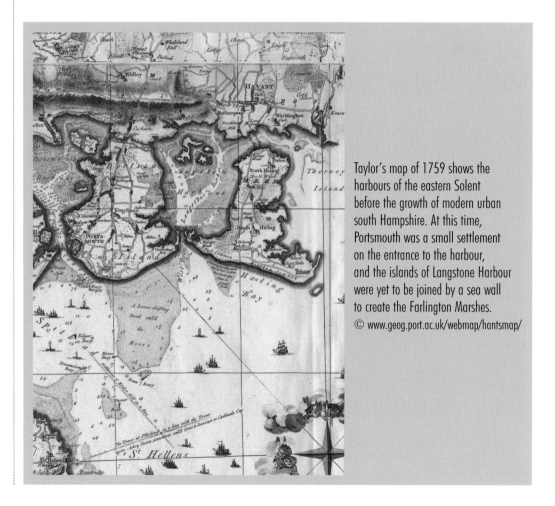

Taylor's map of 1759 shows the harbours of the eastern Solent before the growth of modern urban south Hampshire. At this time, Portsmouth was a small settlement on the entrance to the harbour, and the islands of Langstone Harbour were yet to be joined by a sea wall to create the Farlington Marshes.
© www.geog.port.ac.uk/webmap/hantsmap/

Dave Billett, John Bowers and Graham Rees (left to right) walking across the causeway from "the oysterhouse". © Bill Truckle

In the foreground (left to right) John Bowers and Dave Billett. In the background (left to right) Graham Rees and George Clay. © Bill Truckle

© Keith Brine

The Portsmouth Group

In the years of austerity and reconstruction after the Second World War, a group of Portsmouth schoolboys met at Farlington Marshes to watch, and count, the great flocks of birds visiting the harbours. Over time, they started to co-ordinate the counts. This 'Portsmouth Group' established a methodology of bird counting in estuaries that set a standard that is still used today. The group was made up of remarkable individuals. Dave Billett and Eddie Wiseman went on to be the long-serving wardens at Farlington Marshes and Keyhaven Marshes nature reserves. John Bowers' career took him into university mathematics, his proficiency with figures leading the defence of the great wetlands of Amberley Wildbrooks in Sussex. Another member of the group was Colin Tubbs who became a warden naturalist in the Nature Conservancy. For over thirty years Colin championed the cause of wild nature through his expertise, quiet persuasion and appearances at numerous public inquiries.

The annual beard-grass is a particularly attractive specialist of disturbed ground on Farlington Marshes. The plant was first described in Britain in 1595 from the adjacent Drayton Marshes. The description was made by Richard Garth, a gentleman of Surrey with a particular interest in the commercial value of plants being discovered in the new world of the Americas. © Toni Corelli

By the time the Trust was established in the early 1960s, Farlington Marshes was already recognised as an important wildlife site. The Trust entered into an agreement with the owner to warden the marsh and undertake research. Through the 'great freeze' winter of 1963, the wardens drove crowbars through the frozen ground to erect fences to keep livestock on the marsh. These were lawless years. Assaults on the wardens were not unknown and there was even a shooting. Fortunately for the warden concerned, the majority of the shotgun blast was taken by a birch tree.

By the late 1960s the prospect of maintaining the failing sea wall led to the sale of the marshes to the then Portsmouth County Borough. The Trust continued wardening the marsh, eventually taking on full responsibility for the site.

Although Farlington Marshes is a nature reserve, its special character depends on it being managed as a large grassland farm, grazed by cattle. These marshes have escaped the modern farming techniques that have influenced most other grasslands since the war. As a result, the reserve is incredibly rich both in common wildflowers and insects and in the specialist wildlife of salty pastures. Over 300 species of wildflower are known from the marsh, including more than 50 species of grass.

In early summer cattle are moved onto Farlington Marshes to be fattened on its naturally rich grasslands. © Ian Cameron-Reid

Shelduck breed in disused rabbit holes in the higher, drier parts of the marshes. The birds are present for much of the year, except for mid-summer when they fly to moulting grounds at Heligoland Bight in the German Wadden Sea. In winter the local population swells as birds arrive from all over western Europe. © Tony Wootton

Shut Lake on Farlington Marshes is formed where a small spring-fed stream is held back by the sea wall. The mixture of fresh and brackish water is particularly attractive to birds seeking a safe place to bathe and drink. The seawall provides birdwatchers with clear views across the reeds that surround the lake.
© Jason Crook

Since the Trust first took an interest in Farlington Marshes, the landscape around the reserve has changed dramatically. The north of Langstone Harbour has been developed for waste disposal, playing fields, hotels, shops, warehouses and transport, with the A27 reaching eight lanes in width as it passes through the reserve.

As Farlington has progressively become the last of the great marshes of the Solent Harbours, so wintering birds have become ever more concentrated on its grasslands, and are now found there in globally important numbers. Where spectacular flocks of birds congregate, so do birdwatchers, and Farlington is one of England's premier birdwatching destinations. The reserve is also well-used by the local community, acting as a valued wild space for the people of Portsmouth, one of the mostly densely populated cities in Europe.

The reedbeds and taller grass swamps of the coastal marshes are home to our smallest native mouse, the harvest mouse. The mouse builds its nest amongst the reeds above the level of the summer floods. The harvest mouse's flexible gripping tail helps it to move through the reeds to forage on grass seeds and even an occasional small bird's egg.
© Natalie Rogers

The sea wall around Farlington Marshes offers unrivalled opportunities to see birds. The wall not only overlooks the marshes but also reaches deep into the tidal flats of Langstone Harbour.
© Keith Brine

The importance of Farlington Marshes for wildlife is reflected in an impressive array of national, European and international conservation designations. Though these offer protection 'on paper', the future of the marshes is uncertain. The same forces of nature in action at Lower Test are at play at Farlington Marshes. While the aging sea wall has so far held the rising seas at bay, one day soon it will fail.

The future of Farlington Marshes is in the hands of politicians and engineers. Should the crumbling sea wall be rebuilt? If not, the reserve's amenity value could possibly be recreated elsewhere, but what about the wildlife? In the longer term, it may be possible to find some answers in the other open spaces and wild places of Langstone Harbour. Meanwhile, the Trust will continue its commitment to care for the marshes and help plan for their uncertain future.

Keyhaven and Pennington Marshes nature reserve

In contrast to the urban coasts of the eastern Solent and Southampton Water, the western Solent coast is still comparatively undeveloped. Here, little by little, the Trust has created its largest nature reserve running for over ten kilometres between Hurst Spit and Pitts Deep. This is the Trust's Keyhaven and Pennington Marshes reserve.

In its very first year of existence, the Trust entered into an agreement to warden an area at the end of Hurst Spit. The spit gathers the gravels eroded from Christchurch Bay to create a shingle ridge running some two kilometres into the Solent. In 1961, the Trust was particularly interested in protecting the nesting terns from disturbance. The main colony was fenced and protected from the few people that found their way into what was still a military area. Today the Keyhaven river is busy with leisure craft and the spit has become too popular with people to support large numbers of breeding terns, though a few pairs do attempt to nest each year.

An oystercatcher at sunset.
© Rob Turner

Throughout the late nineteenth century, the saltmarshes of the Keyhaven foreshore expanded out into the Solent. They are now in a state of retreat with marshes turning back into mudflat.
© Mike Read

Yellow horned-poppy. This attractive shingle plant was once known in Hampshire by the local name of squatmore, reflecting its use in traditional herbal medicine to treat bruises ('squat' meaning 'bruise', and 'more' meaning 'root').
© Mark Heighes

A diminutive highlight of Hurst is a tiny geranium, the little robin. A subspecies of this nationally rare plant occurs in the Solent. This dwarf geranium, infused with purple pigments, is found here and nowhere else in the world.
© Clive Chatters

Hurst Spit protects the western Solent from the prevailing south-westerly storms. Within its sheltering arm are extensive mudflats and saltmarshes gradually narrowing towards the mouth of the Beaulieu River. The marshes and shelly spits are not only wintering grounds for migratory birds but also offer safe habitat for nesting seabirds. A huge gullery has grown up on this shore, with thousands of pairs of black-headed gull and, concealed within their midst, growing numbers of Mediterranean gull. The spit itself boasts areas of vegetated shingle, a globally rare habitat.

The flora of shingle is sparse but exceptional. This is a supremely harsh environment where only the specialists tend to prosper.

In common with the rest of the coastline, the marshes and mudflats of the western Solent are changing. The marshes that grew out into the Solent until the 1920s are now shrinking, and as they shrink the mudflats grow; the nature of nature is change.

Dibden Bay

Dibden Bay has gone down in history as the scene of one of the UK's highest profile legal battles over nature conservation. The Bay area is one of the last green expanses on the New Forest coast of Southampton Water. Not only is Southampton Water part of one of the most important wetlands in Europe, it is also one of the most urbanised. Throughout the twentieth century this coast of heathy high ground, woods, fields and saltmarsh has gradually been surrendered to development.

The landscapes that make up Dibden Bay are a mixture of the old and the new. The small, ancient fields and historic grazing marshes of the New Forest National Park run into the great open grasslands of the 'reclaim', a sweep of coastal grassland growing on mud and gravel dredged from Southampton Water. These extensive grasslands are grazed by flocks of estuary ducks in their thousands, and are a prime breeding ground for lapwing. The grasslands in turn give way to the mud of Southampton Water, feeding grounds for the wintering estuary birds and of particular importance at the very lowest tides. The infrequent exposure of the lowest part of the foreshore means that, on the few occasions that this area is available, there is an abundance of food. The whole pattern of landscape is of exceptional interest for wildlife and natural beauty.

Southampton Water is not only of international importance for wildlife but is also the home of one of Britain's biggest container ports and oil refineries. © Dennis Bright

In winter, grey plover fly south from their breeding grounds in western Siberia to the Solent coast. These are birds of wide open spaces that move between the large estuarine foreshores of Hampshire and the Island. At very low tides the broad foreshore of Dibden Bay is a particularly rich feeding ground for these long-distance migrants. © www.brianraffertywildlifephotographer.blogspot.com

Much of Dibden Bay is owned by the port on the opposing shore. In the 1980s, a major housing development was proposed for the Bay and in the 1990s the plans were for port expansion. After a protracted public inquiry, taking over a year and costing tens of millions of pounds, the port proposals were finally rejected by a government inspector and Ministers in 2004.

The Trust played an influential role in the case for more than ten years, promoting the importance of Dibden Bay and its wildlife. For some of those years the Trust stood out against the proposals with support from local ornithologists, other wildlife charities and local residents. As the scientific evidence built up and local opinion became clear, so councils and government agencies joined the Trust in taking a firm stand against port expansion. Ultimately, the campaign bought valuable time for Dibden Bay, but by 2009 plans for port expansion were once again on the table. The case file for Dibden Bay is not yet closed.

The coastal grasslands of Dibden Bay seen from Hythe Marina Village. These grasslands have formed over recent decades on material originally dredged from Southampton Water and placed over the original saltmarshes. The salty soils, coastal location and history of cattle grazing have resulted in habitats that are markedly similar to much older grazing marshes elsewhere in the Solent.
© Dennis Bright

The strong currents in our local seas carry huge quantities of plankton, together with particles of organic matter. This is a bounty for the many kinds of animal that grab, trap or filter their food from the water. In this image, colourful dahlia anemones are surrounded by hornwrack, branching colonies of animals that are frequently mistaken for seaweed.
© Paul Naylor

OUR SEAS

TO A NATURALIST, THE SOLENT does not so much separate the two counties as join them. The birds of the coastal wetlands can be seen crossing from one shore to another as the tides and seasons change. Beneath the water, both counties enjoy an equal share of the marine wildlife within these sheltered waters and beyond them into the open sea.

Much of our sea is shallow, typically no more than 20 metres deep, though in the Hurst Narrows (the narrowest point of the Solent) the seabed descends to 60 metres, and off St Catherine's Point on the Isle of Wight, it is deeper still. Though it is easy to imagine a flat and featureless desert beneath the tides, in reality there is an ever-changing patchwork of dramatic undersea landscapes. There are deep, pebble-lined channels through which the tide races in and out of the harbours. Towering banks of sand and gravel snake their way across the sea floor for many miles. Rocky reefs, ledges, gullies, pinnacles and underwater cliffs bring colour and structure to this world, while submerged caves cry out to be explored. Across this natural landscape, the region's rich maritime past is evident in the scattered remains of many thousands of shipwrecks.

The common hermit crab lives on rocky and sandy seabed. Unlike the rest of its body, the crab's spiral-shaped abdomen lacks a hard shell for protection. Instead, the crab curls its rear end into the depths of an abandoned snail shell, which it then carries around on its back. As the crab grows, it must regularly find a larger shell to occupy. © Paul Naylor

43

Seasquirts are the evolutionary 'missing link' between those animals with backbones and those without. Seasquirt larvae are free-swimming animals that look like tadpoles and have a relatively sophisticated nervous system, including a spinal chord. On reaching maturity, they attach themselves to the seabed and take up a sedentary lifestyle, filtering seawater for food. At this point they digest their spinal chord, which they no longer need.

Right: Lightbulb seasquirts. © Paul Naylor

Below: Gooseberry seasquirts. © Paul Naylor

The Trust's approach to marine conservation

Since its earliest days the Trust has championed coastal conservation, but the wildlife that lives below the tide remained mostly out of sight and out of reach. However, by the end of the 1990s the Trust was committed to becoming involved with wildlife in the sea. Marine conservation requires a somewhat different approach to the Trust's work on land. The Trust cannot buy and manage nature reserves here as, with few exceptions, the seabed belongs to the Crown. The state of knowledge about life in the sea, and of the damage inflicted by decades of mismanagement and neglect, has lagged well behind knowledge of terrestrial wildlife. Until recently, it has not been possible to say where the best places for wildlife are or whether they may need attention.

From the start, the Trust's approach strongly reflected these limitations. Firstly, it was important to find out as much as possible about local marine wildlife, so that the Trust could take an informed position on key issues. Secondly, the Trust sought to understand marine industry and those whose livelihoods depend on the sea, since progress would in many cases be down to their willingness to adapt their practices. Thirdly, there was a need to raise awareness of marine habitats and wildlife, bringing them into the public eye and inspiring others to help protect them. Finally, recognising the scale of the task, the Trust was keen from the outset to work in partnership with others. Indeed, for the first four years from 2000-2004, the main focus was a regional marine programme, which the Trust still co-ordinates on behalf of all the Wildlife Trusts in the South East and in partnership with many other organisations. Only when this programme was well-established did the Trust also commit to local marine conservation projects.

A scuba diver carefully holds a mantis shrimp in a gloved hand. There is good reason for caution – in some parts of the world, mantis shrimps are known as 'thumb-splitters'. © Rohan Holt

Mantis shrimps

The Solent and South Coast Mantis Shrimp Project, which ran from 2002-7, was a novel example of the Trust's approach. The mantis shrimp lives in burrows on the muddy and gravelly seabed of the Solent, This scarce species takes its name from the terrestrial insect, the praying mantis. Like its namesake, the mantis shrimp has two powerful front limbs, held as if in prayer. When a victim comes along, these limbs can strike out with immense speed – almost the fastest acceleration in the animal kingdom – maiming or spearing the unfortunate prey. Local scientist Dr Roger Herbert was keen to study this elusive predator, but was struggling with a shortage of specimens and other records. With funding secured by the Trust, Roger offered a modest bounty to inshore fishermen who occasionally caught the mantis shrimp in their gear. The records – and even live specimens – began to flow in. Meanwhile, the Trust deployed its team of volunteer scuba divers to try to observe the mantis shrimp in its natural habitat, both by day and at night. Through this unusual partnership, the fishermen gained a small bonus, and the Trust gained a leap forward in understanding the ecology and distribution of a fascinating species.

By 2006, survey work conducted by volunteer divers was a central component of the Trust's marine work. Modern sensors and other equipment towed behind a research boat can give a general impression of the seabed, but there is still no substitute for first-hand exploration. Volunteers now dive regularly off our coasts, recording and mapping the full range of natural and manmade habitats, from rocky reefs to shipwrecks, and from gravel banks to eelgrass meadows.

A volunteer scuba diver explores a meadow of thongweed and other seaweeds. One challenge for the Trust's survey work in our local seas is underwater visibility, which can drop to as little as a few centimetres. On a good day though, the volunteer surveyors can enjoy calm, clear seas with over 10 metres of visibility.
© Matt Doggett

Eelgrass is not just interesting for its own sake. These meadows are the habitats where commercial fish such as sea bass — as well as a huge range of other wildlife — have their nurseries. The eelgrass itself is an important food for brent geese and other birds, and the meadows even play a role in protecting our shores from storm damage and coastal erosion. © Paul Kay

Our local seas are home to two species of seahorse, the long-snouted (or spiny) seahorse and the short-snouted seahorse (below). In both species, it is the male that gets pregnant and gives birth to the young. Seahorses mate for life, and couples greet each other each morning with a special 'dance'. © Paul Naylor

Eelgrass meadows

Eelgrass meadows are spread across the Solent's intertidal mudflats and sandflats, as well as in shallow seas beneath the tide. These meadows have been surveyed since the 1960s, with much of the early work done by Colin and Jenni Tubbs. Eelgrass is a true flowering plant that can live out its whole life submerged in seawater, its flowers yielding pollen into the current rather than the breeze. Great meadows of eelgrass have long been known from the Solent, with cyclical declines and recoveries, but the overall trend has been downward and some meadows have disappeared altogether. In 2006, the Trust re-established a survey programme to assess the status of eelgrass in the Solent. Combining a range of techniques, from walking the shore at extreme low tides, to snorkelling, diving and using remote cameras, the Trust has revealed surviving eelgrass meadows in many locations, including exceptional sites along the north-east coast of the Island.

The male corkwing wrasse takes on the lion's share of parental duties. Each male creates a nest in the rocks, lining it with pieces of seaweed. Females tour the reef and each choose a nest in which to lay her eggs. The male then fertilises the eggs and guards them until they hatch. © Robert Bailey

Harbour seals

In 2009, the Trust launched a particularly innovative project, using mobile phone technology to track the Solent's resident harbour seals. The study has revealed some intriguing behaviour. The seals typically rest in Langstone and Chichester Harbours, lounging on the exposed mud banks at low tide, but the animals differ markedly in where they go to feed. The furthest-ranging seal swam to Shoreham on a two-day round trip of 100 miles, sleeping at sea and diving to depths of sixty metres. Three seals regularly ventured to the Isle of Wight, returning on the same day, and there were also frequent trips into Southampton Water. Meanwhile, one seal barely left the shelter of the harbours. The Trust followed up the tagging results by surveying the underwater sites that were visited most frequently by the seals. Knowing more about the seals' feeding grounds and behaviour will be vital if this population is to be properly protected.

The Trust's study of local harbour seals found that they forage primarily in the eastern Solent and in Langstone and Chichester Harbours. It is possible that they feed mainly on flatfish, as harbours and sandy bays are good places to find these. However, some of the seals also hunt in rocky areas, and even around the Solent's underwater anti-submarine barriers, which were built during the Second World War. © Colin Varndell

Next steps in marine conservation

Following the past ten years of intensive effort, the Trust now has a much better understanding of the marine wildlife around our coasts. Thresher sharks are being reported from the deep waters of the English Channel beyond the Isle of Wight, and a 'shark hotspot' frequented by numerous shark species, has been identified to the east of the Island. The Trust's marine mammal reporting scheme has built up a picture of the whales, dolphins, porpoises and seals that use our local seas. In more sheltered waters, Ross corals grow on seabed cobbles and seahorses breed close inshore. What we have discovered in recent years is a tantalising glimpse into the wildlife of our seas, but there are many more mysteries that remain.

It is appropriate that in the 50th anniversary year of the Trust we finally have an Act of Parliament that gives a statutory framework for marine conservation. The Marine & Coastal Access Act, passed in 2009 after a decade-long, UK-wide campaign by The Wildlife Trusts, is now being implemented. Marine Conservation Zones are to be identified and protected by the end of 2012.

Volunteers from The Wildlife Trusts – including Jean Hedley (on the left), President of Hampshire & Isle of Wight Wildlife Trust – lobby outside the Houses of Parliament. This event was part of The Wildlife Trusts' successful ten year campaign for a Marine Act. © RSWT

Opposite: The tompot blenny is found in crevices on rocky reefs and wrecks. This attractive little fish, with its clown-like face, is renowned for its inquisitive nature and is a firm favourite among scuba divers. © Paul Naylor

A number of species of whale, dolphin and porpoise make regular or occasional visits to the seas off Hampshire and the Isle of Wight. These include bottlenose dolphin, common dolphin (left) and long-finned pilot whale. © Caroline Weir / Ketos Ecology

THE ISLE OF WIGHT

FOR ONE OF ENGLAND'S smallest counties, the Island boasts far more than its fair share of wildlife. In essence, the Isle of Wight is a microcosm of lowland southern England, with wonderful examples of many of the typical habitats of the region, frequently with their own Island 'twist'. Within the space of a single day, you can roam over chalk downland, wade through wildflower meadows, step back in time through unspoilt estuaries and ancient woodland, and get your feet wet exploring the Island's spectacular rockpools and sea caves.

The Isle of Wight has been separated from mainland England for only 7,000 years. The few kilometres across the Solent are no barrier to strong swimmers such as otters, nor to bats, birds and flying insects, even those as small as heather beetles. Even so, where differences do exist between the flora and fauna of the Island and the mainland, they can have far-reaching consequences, giving the Island's wild places their own special character.

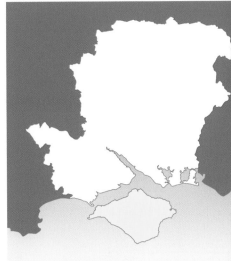

Opposite: The Needles headland is one of the most readily recognised places on the English coast.
© Jackie Cooper

The nationally scarce narrow-leaved lungwort is widely distributed across the north of the Island and on the opposite mainland shore.
© Clive Chatters

53

The Island's flora and fauna

The differences between the bird fauna of the Island and the mainland are subject to change, such as the colonisation of the Island by green woodpeckers in the 1920s.
© Mark Wilson

The Island shares with the adjoining mainland an abundance of the nationally rare narrow-leaved lungwort. This beauty of the spring woods has a British distribution confined to what were, in prehistoric times, the upper tributaries of the Solent river, These tributaries now include the Lymington and Medina rivers. Yet at the same time, other woodland plants that are locally common in Hampshire, such as Solomon's seal and herb Paris, have never been known on the Island.

The bird life of the Island also differs subtly from the mainland. Species relatively common on the mainland have been rare on the Island despite the abundance of what appears to be suitable habitat. The 'twit-twoo' of the tawny owl is not a call readily heard here, in contrast to the adjoining mainland where it is common. Tawny owl habitats on the Island appear to be occupied instead by long-eared owls. Similarly the nuthatch and lesser-spotted woodpecker are almost unknown, and yet they have strongholds on the neighbouring mainland. The habitats on the Island appear suitable yet the birds have not moved in.

Opposite: The 'back of the Wight' is a coastline of farmland and crumbling cliffs where storms and landslips expose world famous fossil beds. Dinosaurs such as Yaverlandia and Iguanodon atherfieldensis are named after the places where they were first found on the Island's coast.
© Jackie Cooper

Three particular absentees – deer, grey squirrel and American mink – have, by their absence, had the greatest impact on the island's wildlife and wild places. Anyone familiar with English woodlands will be immediately struck by the density and vigour of Island coppices. The re-growth from cut stumps may reach well over two metres in the same number of years. The ground flora is dense and deep, knee-high wildflowers thriving in well-lit rides and clearings. This vigour comes from the absence of free-ranging deer. The archaeological record suggests that wild red deer were native on the Island at about the time the Solent separated it from the mainland. These native herds then disappear from the record, possibly hunted to extinction and unable to re-colonise due to the isolation from the mainland herds. There are over a thousand years of documents describing the Island but nowhere is there evidence of herds of deer freely roaming through its woods.

The dormouse has a stronghold on the Island and is known from a variety of woody and scrubby habitats. The earliest record of dormouse in Britain comes from remains found in an archaeological dig in the Island's Undercliff, which were dated to nearly 4,500 years ago.
© Eliana Sevianu

The Bechstein's bat is a creature of the Island's woodlands. It feeds on spiders and resting insects by picking them off twigs and leaves whilst flying by.
© Ian Davidson-Watts

The absence of browsing deer contributes to an abundance of woodland plants and insect life. The insects in turn provide food for an exceptional range of bats. The Island has one of the richest assemblages of bats in Britain, with 14 of Britain's 17 native species. In recent years, great effort has gone into studying and understanding the specialist woodland bats, including the exceedingly rare barbastelle and Bechstein's bats. These two species breed, rest and feed within woodlands and along woodland edges. The countryside of north-east Wight is now recognised as being of international importance for these threatened bats.

The second important absentee is the grey squirrel, allowing the red squirrel to continue to flourish. Red squirrels enjoy a great affection amongst Islanders. The Isle of Wight is the last place in lowland England where red squirrels are abundant in the native broadleaved woodlands that are their natural habitat. Red squirrels have a varied diet of fruit, flowers, insects, fungi and even eggs and nestlings. Diverse native woodland provides all that they need but squirrels are not fussy eaters. Pine cones from introduced conifers will supplement their diet and some squirrels regularly feed from bird tables. In the not too distant past, red squirrels were killed as pests by foresters, for their habit of stripping the bark from young trees. They are now a fully protected species.

Whilst scientists debate the precise details, they all agree that the survival of red squirrels on the Island is the result of the absence of grey squirrels. 'Greys' were introduced into England from North America in 1876 and, by the end of the twentieth century, had all but displaced the native 'reds' throughout lowland England. The spread of 'greys' continues, and unless there is sustained, high-level investment in controlling them, the native 'reds' will eventually be lost from everywhere in Britain other than a few of the smaller islands. The Isle of Wight red squirrel populations are the strongest, and for the time being the safest, in England.

Another species with a safe haven on the Island is the water vole. There has been a steady decline in water vole numbers throughout the UK from as far back as the turn of the 20th century. This decline accelerated from the late 1950s after the accidental introduction of the non-native American mink, a voracious predator, to mainland England. Happily, the Isle of Wight is free from mink – our third absentee – meaning that the Island's water voles are probably the safest population in the whole of the UK.

The red squirrel is a familiar sight in many Island gardens and can be found in most Island woods.
© Ian Pratt

Water voles thrive on the Island due to the absence of American mink.
© Dave Foker

59

Ningwood Common nature reserve

The Trust's Ningwood Common nature reserve, not far from Yarmouth, is the centre of the last population of the reddish buff moth in Britain. This is a moth of wildflower-rich heathy grasslands and was formerly found on the mainland in the New Forest and the Forest of Bere. Saw-wort is the preferred foodplant of the reddish buff caterpillar.

Left: Saw-wort. © Bob Osborn
Below: Reddish buff moth. © Jim Porter
Bottom: Reddish buff caterpillar. © David Green

Trust nature reserves at St Lawrence

The Trust's St Lawrence Bank nature reserve supports one of a handful of populations of field cow-wheat in England. This spectacularly colourful plant is a native of chalky ground and is abundant on the cliffs above the villages of St Lawrence and Niton. In times of less efficient farming, these plants spread into the arable crops of the Island. Whilst today we may enjoy the flowering of a flamboyant weed, the Islanders in the past called it 'poverty weed', as it contaminated the grain crop and tainted the flour. Labourers were paid to pull it from the fields before harvest-time.

Here at St Lawrence is the Trust's only arable field nature reserve. Unlike the farmers of the past, the Trust is looking forward to cow-wheat spreading from its field-side bank into the arable crop. An arable nature reserve is unusual, and offers interesting opportunities to fit nature into the Island's rural economy. Rather than standing apart from the life of the local community, the field provides a perfect venue for the Island's vintage tractor owners to practice their skills.

Field cow-wheat grows in naturally open habitats on the Island's cliffs as well as in the bare ground created by farming. The seeds of this plant have a small oil capsule at one end, which attracts ants. It is thought that ants carry the seeds to their nests and eat the oil, leaving the seed itself to germinate. © Alice Stoecklin, Switzerland

Vintage tractors ploughing the Trust's field at St Lawrence.
© Chris Archbold

The naturally maintained open habitats of the Undercliff at Niton. The Trust's St Lawrence Undercliff nature reserve is nearby.
Credit: © Jackie Cooper

Opposite: The Glanville fritillary is one of the Island's specialities. The caterpillars feed on the leaves of ribwort plantain that grows on the regularly disturbed soils of coastal landslips. © Ian Pratt

Trust members crossing an extensive mudslide whilst surveying the Undercliff.
© Clive Chatters

St Lawrence Bank is perched on a cliff top. The cliff drops some 40 metres, not into the sea but into the village of St Lawrence. This part of the Island is geologically highly active with numerous 'benches' and 'hollows' stretching over half a kilometre between the cliffs and the sea. This is known as the Undercliff, a landscape as beautiful as it is uncertain. The villagers of the Undercliff live in one of Europe's largest rotational landslips. What brings uncertainty to the local community also brings opportunities for wildlife.

The most regular landslips produce a constant supply of sunny bare ground. A highly specialised community of insects lives within this reliably unstable habitat. These include a range of bees and wasps, craneflies, weevils and bugs. Prominent amongst these creatures is the Glanville fritillary butterfly, which is found throughout this coastline. These strong populations sometimes spill out to temporarily colonise other sites, even as far afield as the Hampshire coast. The woodlands that the Trust owns in the Undercliff are home to scarce native plants of warm humid conditions, such as the Italian lords-and-ladies together with the parasitic ivy broomrape.

The Island's countryside is highly diverse with a variety of farming systems. © Graham Drucker

Working with the farming community

The Trust is a substantial landowner across the two counties, even within the context of the large country estates of England. However, the land that the Trust directly manages is a tiny proportion of the countryside, and that will always be the case. This is particularly true on the Island.

Most land on the Island is in private ownership and is farmed by family businesses. In times past, wildlife and a beautiful countryside were the fortunate by-products of a traditionally farmed landscape. Through the twentieth century, the technical revolution in the agricultural industry greatly improved productivity at the expense of many habitats and species. As the Trust reaches its 50th anniversary, the future of wildlife in the farmed countryside is not something that can be left to chance.

An arable field in the east Wight ablaze with poppies. © Jackie Cooper

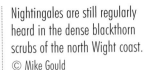

Nightingales are still regularly heard in the dense blackthorn scrubs of the north Wight coast.
© Mike Gould

Since the 1940s, British agriculture has been supported by various grants and subsidies. In recent years, a proportion of this financial support has been directed towards environmental initiatives. These schemes not only promote wildlife but also other important environmental matters such as soil conservation and the improvement of water quality. The Trust's expertise and local knowledge has assisted 162 farm businesses to obtain environmental grants in recent years, helping them to manage over 30% of the Island's land surface in a wildlife-friendly way.

One of the options available to farmers is to plant trees. In most cases tree planting is not the most obvious way to enhance wildlife. Indeed, over the nineteenth and twentieth centuries, well-meaning but inappropriate tree planting in the UK has caused immense damage to habitats such as chalk grasslands and heathlands. On the Island, however, the Trust promotes tree planting for the benefit of the exceptional woodland mammals.

Species such as woodland bats, dormice and red squirrels benefit from carefully sited tree planting schemes that link up isolated areas of woodland. The re-planting of a hedgerow can create a corridor between woods, which mammals use to feed, breed and found new colonies. In recent years the Trust has supported Isle of Wight farmers in planting and reinforcing some 500 kilometres of hedgerow, together with creating 220 hectares of new woodland.

THE NEW FOREST AND THE AVON VALLEY

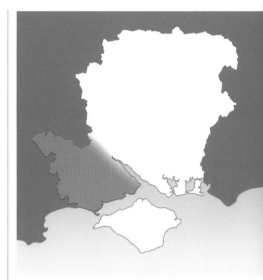

T HE SOUTH-WEST OF HAMPSHIRE is one of the richest areas in Britain for wildlife. This is a landscape of superlatives. Here are over 15,000 hectares of lowland heath and bog, the largest area of these habitats anywhere in Britain. Within the same area is the largest expanse of ancient pasture woodland in the lowlands, at over 4,600 hectares. This rich tapestry of ancient oak and beech woods, mires and bogs, meandering gravel-bottomed streams, wet woods, seasonal ponds and windswept open heathland represents a vast interconnected mosaic of unparalleled diversity. Nowhere else in Europe do these habitats occur together in such a large area. The New Forest's importance for wildlife is also demonstrated by its legal protection under domestic and international law – and its recent designation as a National Park.

The New Forest of today grew out of ancient hunting grounds of the Saxon kings. In 1079 the conquering Normans decided to call the area 'New' and the name stuck for the following 900 years. The term 'Forest' in the eleventh century did not imply an area covered by trees. Forests were subject to forest law as well as the law of the land, the extra layer of administration safeguarding the interests of the King. Today's New Forest still contains many of the landscapes and modern versions of the rural economy and legal system that would have been familiar to our Saxon and Norman forebears.

The unenclosed areas (known as the Open Forest) make up one large grazing unit, locally dissected by fenced roads and timber plantations. This single connected block of land runs from the saltmarsh foreshore of the Lymington River up into the floodplain of the Avon by the village of Woodgreen. The open country and ancient woods of the New Forest so dominate the landscape that it is all too easy to overlook the area's other exceptional places for wildlife including the farmland, the coast and the river valleys.

Chamomile is widespread across the Forest on hard-grazed lawns and village greens. © Sonja Ehlen

Opposite: Ancient beech trees at Vinney Ridge. The open-grown shape of these trees is a result of youthful trees in sunny glades being cut for small wood high above the reach of grazing animals. © Mike Read

Within the broad landscapes are multiple quirks which give detail and diversity to the area. The concrete rubble of abandoned aerodromes is now home to species usually associated with chalk grassland, such as salad burnet and small blue butterflies. The remains of an old bombing range have Hampshire's strongest population of the early gentian, another specialist of lime-rich places.

Within the heathlands, once pared by local people for their home-fire turf, are stands of marsh clubmoss and brown-beaked sedge. The botanically uninspiring timber plantations support strong and growing populations of firecrest and goshawk. The fresh heathers of recently burnt heathland are alive with grayling, dark-green fritillary and silver-studded blue butterflies. The Open Forest still functions as an intact landscape, and offers a model of what we wish to achieve elsewhere in the future.

Common cotton-grass (left) and bog asphodel (right) are found across the wet heaths and bogs of the Open Forest. © Peter Durnell

Above left: Wild gladioli were first discovered in Britain on the Isle of Wight in 1855, then a year later in the New Forest and later still in Dorset. The Island and the Dorset populations have died out following habitat destruction. Gladioli are still scattered across the richer soils of the Open Forest, growing amongst bluebells and wood anemones within bracken heaths. © Peter Durnell

Above right: The pale butterwort is common across the Forest in scuffed wet heaths and amongst bog pools. The leaves have an unhealthy pallour, the in-rolled leaf edges trapping small insects in glistening slime. This is one of many insect-eating plants of the Forest's wetlands, where nutrients are hard to come by. © Peter Durnell

When the Trust was founded in the early 1960s, the New Forest was under intense pressure. Plantation forestry was replacing ancient woodlands, heaths and bogs. Groves of ancient trees were being cleared away and deep drains cut through precious wetlands. All along the eastern borders of the Forest, heavy industry was expanding across the estuary of Southampton Water and the Waterside towns rapidly grew out from historic villages.

At the same time a more subtle change was taking place. This change was to the pastoral rural economy that defines the Forest and which for centuries has supplied the animals that graze its open spaces. The wildlife that makes the New Forest special is substantially dependant on Forest habitats being grazed. The New Forest pony has rightly been called 'the architect of the Forest'. Animals are put out to graze the Open Forest by commoners who exercise ancient rights. These ancient rights in turn are tied to properties, both houses and fields.

The commoning way of life is typically a marginal existence. Income from rearing livestock is no match for the wealth that can be earned in towns and cities. With the growth of urban areas surrounding the Forest and the increasing suburbanisation of the Forest itself, it has become increasingly difficult for people living the commoning way of life to compete on the open market for fields to rent or homes to live in. The Trust was one of the first organisations to recognise that the exceptional wildlife of the Forest was at risk if the rural economy of the Forest faltered.

Opposite: Ponies at Howen Bottom near Fritham. © Mike Read

The sale yard at Beaulieu Road Station where Forest ponies are auctioned every autumn and spring. © Nigel Matthews, New Forest National Park Authority

Roydon Woods nature reserve and the Barker-Mill legacy

In 1966 a part of the Roydon Estate, south of Brockenhurst, came up for sale. Described as *"300 acres in three parcels of heather and natural re-seeded Scots pine"*, this was part of the former Setley Common. The seemingly exorbitant asking price at that time was £100 an acre. As much as the Trust wished to buy this land, the Trustees concluded that it was not affordable.

Setley Common at Roydon.
© Mike Read

The woods at Roydon are crossed
by many ancient trackways.
© Eleanor Wilkins

Peter Barker-Mill in his studio.
© Tony Boxall

In May 1977, Peter Barker-Mill was contemplating the future of some of his estates. Peter had become aware of the wildlife value of his recently purchased land at Roydon through conversations with Colin Tubbs. He was also familiar with the Trust, as the family was the Trust's landlord at the Lower Test Marshes nature reserve. Peter wanted to do what was right for the land, and so opened a discussion with the Trust with a view to leasing around 280 hectares. Ultimately, these discussions culminated in Peter expressing his wish to give the whole estate to the Trust: 950 acres of wood, heath and farmland, together with much of the Lymington River. The scale and generosity of the gift was astounding.

The Trust was used to owning land but Roydon was something different. Here was a fair-sized country estate, bringing with it a dozen farming tenants, a fishing club and farmland as well as a substantial area of ancient woodland. Over time, the management of the estate settled down to a pragmatic approach overseen by the daily decisions of Michael Boxall, the Trust's warden on the site from 1984 to the present day. Here is a place with endless demands for maintaining hedges and fences, for overseeing contractors and assisting visitors.

The worked coppices by the river at Roydon are some of the last few places in the New Forest where the woods are regularly cut and the deer populations held in check. In the well-lit glades, free from browsing deer, are flower-rich woodland floors with bastard balm and narrow-leaved lungwort. Drifts of violets in the coppiced woods provide a habitat for caterpillars of the silver-washed fritillary and the much rarer pearl-bordered fritillary, which is an occasional visitor to the rides.

Elsewhere in Roydon are more typical Forest landscapes of grazed woodlands of ancient trees, wildflower meadows, heaths and bogs, all intertwined within an ancient landscape of former fields and homesteads.

Violets carpet the floor of the coppiced woods at Roydon. © Ken Dolbear

Roydon Woods is alive with silver-washed fritillaries through the summer. © Jon Oakley

The Lymington Reedbeds.
© Mike Read

Over the years the estate has grown, with the addition of land in the Lymington Valley, the Lymington Reedbeds (following a public appeal) and, most recently, some areas of heathland at Sandy Down.

Roydon played an important part in the Trust growing to recognise that conserving wildlife was about more than just fighting off harmful developments and managing nature reserves. At Roydon, the Trust had fields of unexceptional value to nature in their own right. Yet, by choosing the 'right' tenant and setting a sensible rent, the Trust found it was able to support local people whose lives in turn supported the Forest. The Trust decided to rent out its farmland to local commoners at an agricultural rent. Here they could make hay to provide winter feed for the cattle and ponies that graze the commons of the Forest for the rest of the year. The Trust's relationship with the commoners and the rural economy of the Forest had fundamentally changed.

New Forest woodland is characterised by an abundance of sunny glades (which benefit wild flowers and sun-loving insects) and dead wood (which provides a habitat for fungi and specialist invertebrates). © Robert Chapman

Mud, dung and decay

The New Forest is particularly rich in wildlife that was once common. As ancient farming methods have declined elsewhere, so the Forest grows in importance for the species that live in mud, dung and decaying matter. Over the years, the Trust has undertaken many surveys of these extraordinary species in their increasingly rare habitats. These projects enabled the Trust to corral the skill and dedication of volunteer naturalists and provide data-rich reports which have proved very influential. Studying these unusual species and their highly specific habitats added to the collective understanding of the importance of continuing the Forest's ancient management methods.

Unlike everyday supermarket mushrooms, the tooth fungi have spines instead of gills. The ancient woods of the New Forest are a national stronghold for this spectacular group of fungi, but even here they are found sporadically in just two-dozen or so locations.

Every autumn the decaying trunks of dead beech trees are festooned with the ivory coralline spines of the tooth fungus (*Hericium coralloides*).
© Paul Hugill

The hornet robber-fly depends on grazed grassland and heath, as animal dung plays an important part in its lifecycle. The adults are predatory, intercepting their prey in mid-flight. They favour dung beetles but also take grasshoppers, bees and wasps. Females lay their eggs in animal dung and the larvae, which are also predatory, feed on dung beetle grubs and burrow into the soil before pupating.
© Linda Priestley

The nail fungus (*Poronia punctata*) is widespread across the pony-grazed heaths of the Forest. The fruiting bodies of the fungus appear on the surface of partially decayed pony dung throughout the year but are most abundant when the ground is warm and damp.
Left: © Stuart Skeates
Right: © Peter Hogan

The dung of the Forest's ponies and cattle provides a rich habitat important for fungi, flies and beetles, which in turn feed mammals and birds. With several thousand grazing animals feeding on a diet rich in organic roughage, the Forest supports an impressive diversity of species dependent on abundant dung.

The grazing animals themselves can become food. Within the ponds of the south of the Forest is Britain's largest leech, the medicinal leech. An adult leech can grow to some 20 centimetres and is now a very rare species in Britain. For most of their lives the leeches live in ponds, taking opportunities to feed on their neighbours. A particularly gruesome sight is a mass of mating frogs, some of which look partially deflated by leeches. When ponies and cattle come to the ponds to drink they offer a chance for leeches not only to feed but also to latch on and so move from pond to pond.

There are many hundreds of ponds throughout the Forest, about half of which dry up in most years. These seasonal ponds provide the perfect habitat for a variety of species that can survive the extremes of wetting and drying. The largest of these is the *Triops*, a bizarre ancient crustacean that has only been found in Britain in a handful of ponds. The British population appears to consist entirely of self-fertile females.

Much more widespread in Forest ponds are fairy shrimps. Like the *Triops* they can hatch from eggs laid in the drying mud to grow rapidly into fully mature adults. Their ability to withstand harsh conditions is remarkable: adults can survive beneath the frozen surface of the pond in winter, and in summer they can 'turn on' red blood cells as oxygen levels decline in the heat.

Where you find fairy shrimps, you may also find the late summer flowers of pennyroyal mint, chamomile and small fleabane. These traditional plants of village greens were once quite common across lowland England. With so many greens and commons elsewhere in Britain no longer being grazed, so the habitats have changed and we are left with a simpler and less diverse flora.

The River Avon and its wide floodplain, seen here from Castle Hill in the New Forest. © Mike Read

The Avon Valley

Towards the Hampshire border with Dorset, the high heathy ground of the New Forest falls away into the broad floodplain of the Hampshire Avon. The Avon is one of the great rivers in England, rising to the north of Salisbury Plain then flowing southward, fed by the Plain's great chalk aquifer and the streams of the Forest.

The Avon supports one of the most diverse fish faunas of any English river, with at least 29 native fish including salmon, lamprey, bullhead and brown trout. Within the river are over 60 species of water plant. As well as the classic water crowfoot communities of other chalk rivers, the muddy grazed backwaters of the Avon are home to mudwort and frogbit.

The Valley still regularly floods, depositing nutrient-rich silt across the grasslands to maintain their natural fertility. Within these fertile floodlands are occasional raised areas of gravel and sand, within which heathland and even sand dune species can be found. Where traditional hay cutting and pasture farming persist, the Valley still excels in supporting flocks of wintering waterfowl such as wigeon, teal, and gadwall, together with waders such as black-tailed godwit, redshank and lapwing.

By the time the river reaches Blashford, the gin-clear, chalk-fed waters of the Avon are mixed with the sherry-tinted heathland streams of the Forest. Between the heaths of the Forest and the floodplain of the river is a broad stretch of level ground, an ancient river terrace laid down in a past ice age.

These flat terraces have a long history of human use. Here may be found assemblages of tools from the Old Stone Age, up to half a million years old. Within living memory, the land around Blashford has changed from farmland to a military aerodrome, and then been worked as a gravel pit before eventually becoming a Trust nature reserve.

The development of Blashford Lakes

From the mid 1970s, the Trust started making representations to planners on the future of an area of land earmarked for gravel extraction, close to Blashford. Through the next two decades, the wildlife potential of the mineral workings in the Avon was championed by Mike Read of the Ringwood Natural History Society. A local man and keen birdwatcher, Mike realised that mineral extraction, which was widely perceived as a threat to the tranquillity of the countryside, could pave the way for something special being created afterwards. He convinced the Wildlife Trust and the Nature Conservancy Council of his vision, and they in turn promoted it to the relevant local authorities. In this vision, Blashford Lakes would be re-born as a superb, tailor-made wetland complementing both the Avon Valley and the New Forest. As well as spectacular wildlife, the lakes could offer quiet enjoyment for a range of water sports, fishing and as an amenity for Ringwood and the growing towns of south-east Dorset.

Opposite: Black-tailed godwit congregate in the lower Avon Valley where the river flows from Hampshire into Dorset. © John Windust

Ivy Lake, viewed from the south hide at Blashford Lakes nature reserve. © Karen White

Left: The reedbeds of Blashford Lakes are frequently visited by over-wintering bittern. © Tony Bates, chalto.co.uk

Right: Golden-ringed dragonflies breed in the Forest streams and fly over the whole of the Blashford Lakes nature reserve. © Elliott Fairs

The beewolf hunts down honeybees and feeds the paralysed prey to its young. The open sandy grasslands at Blashford Lakes are an ideal habitat for this sun-lover. © Robert Chapman

Lichen heaths have formed on the raw soils of the former gravel works at Blashford Lakes. © Robert Chapman

The brook lamprey is a primitive, jawless fish resembling an eel. It spawns in clean gravel beds in rivers where the current is not too strong.
© Petr Mückstein

It was good fortune that the lakes being created by the gravel workings were also of interest to other bodies. The privatisation of the water industry in the late 1980s brought with it a period of strategic investment. Water companies saw opportunities at Blashford Lakes for securing a water supply for their customers. At the same time, the local authority saw the benefit of providing open space for the community. The Trust's vision was wholly compatible with these other uses and the Blashford Lakes of today was born.

Habitat improvements at Blashford Lakes continue. In 2005, the Trust undertook a dramatic restoration of the Dockens Water stream, moving vast quantities of earth to reinstate the natural twists and turns that had been artificially straightened during the construction of the former airfield. This river restoration project was a quiet success, with the brook lamprey recolonising the newly restored stream within days of the work finishing.

A family of great crested grebes nesting on the lake margins.
© Robert Chapman

Over the years, Blashford Lakes has grown both in its importance and its value for people from local communities and further afield. A network of paths has been built to accommodate all visitors, including those with children's buggies and mobility scooters. This is a big site – two kilometres from end to end and over a kilometre wide – easily a place to enjoy a full day in the countryside.

At the heart of Blashford Lakes is the education centre. Each year, thousands of school children pass through its doors and are introduced to the natural world in all its wet, muddy and prickly glory. After-hours events share the skill of cooking on a camp fire or the thrill of sitting quietly in the dark, waiting for the badgers to arrive.

Pond dipping beside the education centre. © Sally Hayns

The hobby is one of the New Forest's very special birds. With distinctive rusty-brown 'trousers' and sharply pointed wings, it is an elegant creature. Arriving in the New Forest from its African wintering grounds in mid-April, hobbies can regularly be seen over heaths and bogs, hawking for insects — dragonflies are favourites — that are often taken and devoured on the wing. © Mike Read.

Opposite: Sunset on the Open Forest. © Matt Doggett

THE HAMPSHIRE CHALKLANDS

THE TOWNS AND CITIES of south Hampshire are separated from those in the north by a broad swathe of countryside. Much of this land overlies chalk, a soft white limestone. The chalk gives rise to thin alkaline soils which support specialised plants, and provides huge aquifers which store most of our water, feeding the great chalk rivers for which this part of the world is renowned.

Today, the Hampshire chalk country is mainly a landscape of large arable farms, but it would be wrong to underestimate the value of this stretch of countryside for wildlife. Here is a remarkable concentration of ancient woods (mostly hazel coppices), fragments of exceptionally rich chalk grasslands and fen meadows in the river valleys, all relics of historic farming practices.

Before the advent of artificial chemical fertilisers, sheep were used to prepare land for growing cereals. Vast flocks were grazed on the downland pastures and on the sweet fen meadows of the river valleys. The sheep were closely shepherded and penned on the arable fields so that their dung would transfer the natural fertility of the grassland to the grain field. The hazel copses of the chalk country provided the raw materials to make the hurdles essential for managing the flocks. So it was that the different habitats of the chalklands were linked together through traditional agricultural management.

Opposite: Springtime in a chalk pasture with cowslips and early purple orchids.
© Mark Heighes

The sword-leaved helleborine is
a woodland orchid with a national
stronghold in east Hampshire.
© Tim Ford

Shutts Copse and Chappetts Copse nature reserves

The Trust's Shutts Copse nature reserve lies between the headwaters of the rivers Itchen and Meon. Shutts Copse is typical of the ancient woodlands of the chalk. It has a quiet beauty of its own with a brief but spectacular flowering of bluebells, wood anemones and Solomon's seal wherever the wood has been recently coppiced. The older hazel stands are home to dormice and so the Trust's management strikes a balance between the botanical advantages of the cutting of the woods and the benefits to mammals of tall hazel.

Shutts Copse was given to the Trust in the late 1980s by the Honourable Miss Joane Dutton of Hinton Ampner. The gift was a part of a much larger legacy which throughout the 1990s underwrote the Trust's rapid development to be the organisation that it is today. Miss Dutton's generosity is commemorated each year through the award of the Dutton Prize, given to volunteers who have made an exceptional contribution to the work of the Trust.

Chappetts Copse, a similar wood on the edge of the Meon Valley, was given to the Trust in 1981 by Edith Whitehead. Since then, Trust volunteers under the leadership of Richard Hedley have managed the wood so it supports the largest population of sword-leaved helleborine orchids in the country.

Coppice management at Shutts Copse provides open glades as well as dappled shade, bringing light to the woodland floor.
© Albert Roberts

Wildlife of the arable chalk

As farming techniques have become more productive so there is less space for wildlife. However, even arable land need not be a wildlife-free zone. The inefficiencies of traditional farming left gaps in the crops where wildflowers could grow. Species such as the pheasant's-eye, a filigree-foliaged red buttercup, are now very rare. Stone curlew that nest on open ground amongst crops are vulnerable to machinery and to the pesticides that suppress their insect food. Both species respond well to conservation farming and can still be seen within Hampshire's chalkland.

Left: Pheasant's-eye. © Eduardo Duro

Below: Stone curlew. © Robert Pickett, Papiliophotos.com

Sheep grazing on Broughton Down.
© Jon Oakley

Broughton Down nature reserve

The high quality habitats of the Hampshire chalk tend to be found as islands within the farmed landscape. Such an island is Broughton Down.

One of the most extraordinary things about Broughton Down is that it is there at all. Until the late eighteenth century the parish of Broughton was managed as a series of commons. What we call Broughton Down today was a part of 'Old Down', one of the four downland pastures of the parish. In 1789 all of the commons were enclosed by Act of Parliament which resulted in their redistribution as the private property of 51 beneficiaries. Unlike the other downland pastures of the parish, Broughton Down was not ploughed following enclosure, nor was it planted with trees. The extreme steepness of the slopes would have discouraged attempts to break up the ancient turf and the value of the pastures would have meant it was only worth keeping for grazing. By the time the Trust obtained a substantial part of the Down from the Sainsbury family in 1984, the value of the grazing was low and the site was threatened by the invasion of scrub. Since then, the Trust's management has restored the open grassland.

Right: Silver-spotted skipper.
© Jon Oakley

Below: Dodder.
© floralimages.co.uk

Bottom: Bastard toadflax.
© Ken Dolbear

On a hot summer's day Broughton Down sparkles with butterflies. Thirty-two species of butterfly breed here. One of these is the silver-spotted skipper, a sun-loving creature of bare open hillsides and a specialist of the southern English chalk; its caterpillars feed on tufts of sheep's fescue grass in the heat of broken turf. By the early 1980s silver-spotted skipper populations in England were in rapid decline. In the national census of 1983, Broughton Down was identified as having the strongest population in England. Since the re-establishment of grazing on chalk grasslands elsewhere in England, there has been a modest, but very encouraging, recovery of populations nationally. Broughton Down provided a safe refuge for the silver-spotted skipper and a springboard for its recovery across the wider landscape.

The Down is home to two species of plant that parasitise their neighbours to gain nourishment. Red waxy filaments of parasitic dodder drape the rockroses and thymes that grow around the pre-historic burial mounds on the downland crest. For most of its life dodder is a plant without leaves or roots or any green parts. It is totally parasitic, concentrating all its growth into extracting the nutrients from its hosts to flower, set seed and so establish the next generation.

Unlike dodder, the bastard toadflax has some green leaves and makes a contribution towards its own upkeep whilst also parasitising its neighbours. If enjoying the toadflax's tiny 'stars-in-the-grass' flowers is not a sufficient forensic delight, then even closer diligence will reveal a tiny dark blue shield bug sucking on toadflax sap. This shield bug is a specialist of bastard toadflax.

In exceptionally rich and ancient places such as Broughton Down, wild nature can be enjoyed at a variety of scales. The hill top views, looking over the widening plain across north-west Hampshire into Wiltshire, are exceptional. In contrast, a closer focus reveals endless layers of complexity of life.

A view across Broughton Down to the ancient burial mound on its crest, known locally as the 'Plum Pudding'.
© Brian Shorter

Right: Water crowfoot is a classic chalk stream species. Favouring fast-flowing water, it provides a habitat for fly life and other aquatic invertebrates.
© Lawrence Talks

Below: The River Itchen is one of the world's finest chalk streams, with gravelly beds, clear water, and prolific growth of water crowfoot. The whole river system is highly valued for its plant, invertebrate, mammal, bird and fish communities.
© Graham Roberts

The chalk rivers

The chalk hills of Hampshire are porous and winter rain percolates through them to form great underground reservoirs of clean fresh water. In places, water spills out as chalk springs and winterbournes to form the headwaters of our chalk rivers. Such springs can be seen at the Trust's Greywell Moors nature reserve, where the fen and the River Whitewater are fed by a constant source of crystal clear water.

Chalk rivers have been described as "as clear as gin, and twice as expensive". The high commercial value of these waters reflects their potential for sport fisheries, as they are the natural habitat of salmon and trout. The clear water supports aquatic plant communities that are of international importance. The '*Ranunculus* community' dominated by water crowfoot, water starwort, watercress and water parsnip, forms the basis of this finely balanced ecosystem, supporting the fly life that in turn is food for fish and other species.

The ragged robin is a member of the carnation family and is found in high quality fens and wetland meadows of our chalk river valleys. © David Kilbey

Kingfishers are found along Hampshire's chalk river valleys. Nesting in tunnels excavated into sandy river banks, they are expert fish catchers. Wandering along one of our quieter riversides, you may be lucky enough to see an unmistakable flash of metallic blue and orange as a kingfisher dives like an arrow to spear a fish with its dagger-like beak.
© Andy Browne

The valleys of the chalk rivers are naturally fertile in comparison with the thin soils through which they flow. From the seventeenth century onwards, where there was sufficient gradient, the natural fen-grassland of the valleys was converted into water meadows. Water meadows were engineered landscapes designed to bring the warm waters of the river onto the land to irrigate and defrost the valley grasslands, giving an early bite to the great sheep flocks of the downs.

Today a few relic water meadows remain, and those which are managed with extensive grazing systems support exceptionally rich wildlife. Conventional farming has become the major land use for much of the river valleys or, where land ownership has become fragmented, the fields are turning into rank grassland and scrubland. The Trust has worked with landowners in the chalk river valleys for over 20 years to improve habitat management for wildlife.

The southern damselfly is associated with the well-vegetated flowing backwaters of the river valley fen-meadows. Hampshire is a national stronghold of these spectacular blue insects. The chalk stream valleys of the Itchen and Test together with the wetlands of the New Forest are recognised as supporting internationally important populations.
© Ben Rushbrook

The Trust's involvement with landowners in the chalk river valleys began with the otter. From the 1950s through to the 1980s, populations of otters in England's rivers were in rapid decline. A combination of habitat destruction and inadvertent poisoning by pesticides had reduced the once-widespread otter to a rare and threatened species. By the late 1980s the upper Itchen Valley was one of the few places in southern England where otters survived.

Otter surveys in the 1980s and 90s introduced the Trust to privately owned stretches of the Rivers Itchen and Test. Surveying the secretive otter requires patience and skill. The creatures themselves are rarely seen but they leave territorial marks of mounds of musky-scented faeces known as sprint, which is relatively easy to collect. Over the years these surveys built relationships which led to habitat improvements and practical solutions to problems. Today otters are using all available suitable habitats across Hampshire's rivers; their recovery has been a quiet success.

Opposite: The otter is our largest native land carnivore. A fully grown dog otter may reach 1.2 metres in length and weigh over 12 kilograms. These large animals need big territories, with a dog otter using up to 40 kilometres of river. Feeding on fish and crustaceans, otters need a combination of excellent water quality, interconnected habitats and quiet lying-up and breeding areas — often in areas of wet woodland.
© Chris Bean

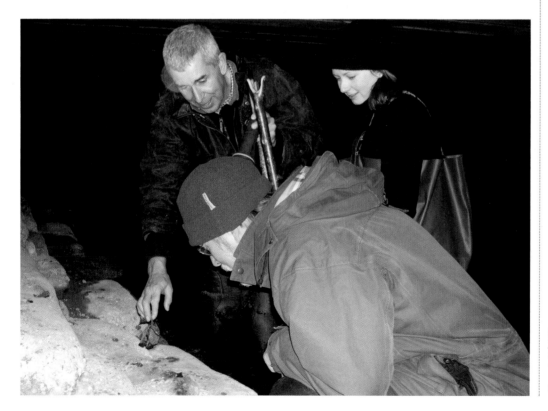

Graham Roberts (top left), the Trust's Otters and Rivers Officer from 1989-2010, collecting otter sprint.
© Elliott Fairs

The advice and support that the Trust gives to private landowners along the river valleys seeks to address their needs as well as those of the wildlife. A Trust advisor has no authority but is able to help sort out problems of water quality or soil erosion without the landowner fearing the heavy hand of bureaucracy. Whilst doing so, improvements for wildlife are built in, for example some delighted landowners are enjoying the return of breeding lapwing to the restored floodplain meadows after years of absence. In recent years our project officers have worked discreetly through the valleys of the Loddon and Lyde, Whitewater, Meon, Test, Itchen and Avon. Over the years, trust and mutual respect are won and so the countryside and the rural economy are enhanced.

The tumbling cries of nesting lapwing are a thrilling reward for restoring floodplain meadows.
© Darin Smith

Opposite: Where mink numbers are controlled by fishery interests, water voles are thriving. © Tony Wootton

Greywell Moors nature reserve

Southern marsh orchid.
© David Kilbey

Greywell Moors is one of the few places in lowland Britain where you can still enjoy unspoilt springhead fen habitats. The headwaters of the River Whitewater bubble up through the peaty soils, depositing calcium carbonate and locking up phosphates. This provides nutrient-poor conditions which support rare and specialist plants, despite being surrounded by a modern farmed landscape drenched in fertilisers. This small and fragile reserve is rich in classic wetland species such as marsh helleborine, southern marsh orchid, great fen-sedge and lesser tussock-sedge. Its exceptional fenland 'brown moss' community is revered throughout the nation by bryologists, specialists in these plants. The site was first recognised by naturalists in the late nineteenth century and was listed on the seminal Rothschild list of important sites, produced at the time of the First World War. The Trust acquired the reserve in 1989 and dedicated it to the great bryologist Ted Wallace who, along with other naturalists, studied Greywell's special flora during the 1920s and 30s. Today, its small size and isolation are a threat, as is water abstraction. Maintaining the reserve's interest is an ongoing management challenge for the Trust.

Cattle grazing at Greywell Moors.
© Jon Oakley

Rising near Basingstoke, the River Loddon is a chalk stream tributary of the Thames. The Loddon Valley has its own distinct flora including the Loddon lily. Where the river crosses the county boundary into Berkshire, the springtime meadows are host to a rare population of snakes-head fritillary. This stretch of river is also home to the highly localised Loddon pondweed.

Left: Snakes-head fritillary. © Simon Booth
Above: Loddon lily. © Clive Philips

Opposite: The northern meadows of Winnall Moors have been sensitively farmed for decades and produce fine sweet hay as well as being an exceptional habitat for wetland wildlife.
© Steve Page

The pyramidal orchid is one of the most widespread grassland orchids of the South Downs.
© Mark Heighes

A gateway to the South Downs National Park

A towering statue of King Alfred, Alfred the Great, stands at the bottom of Winchester High Street. Alfred was King of Wessex and, in his time, Winchester was the capital of his Kingdom and, in later years, of the Kingdom of England. Some of the streets that Alfred laid out over the former Roman town of Venta Belgarum are those that serve Winchester city centre today. These reflect the line of the ancient defensive walls, within which were fortified gates such as the great medieval West Gate at the opposite end of the High Street to Alfred's statue. A much more discreet gate, a postern gate, passed through the eastern wall at what is known today as Durngate.

Durngate is now a gateway to the countryside of the South Downs National Park. After some 60 years of debate, the National Park was established in April 2010 and runs for over 110 kilometres from the heart of Winchester to the chalk cliffs of Beachy Head. The countryside that leads out of the city from Durngate is the entrance to Winnall Moors, a Trust nature reserve that safeguards an important area of river valley wetlands.

Winnall Moors nature reserve

Winnall Moors nature reserve encompasses a large section of the River Itchen and its floodplain, extending a mile upstream of central Winchester. Steeped in medieval history, the area within the reserve has been profoundly shaped by the water meadow system which dominated Hampshire's river valleys in previous centuries. The water meadows and their carriers (irrigation channels) were constructed in the 1670s and managed traditionally until the 1930s, making it one of the last systems to operate in the Itchen Valley. The area is also of historic importance for fly-fishing, and the renowned Abbots Barton fishery is very much a part of what is now the Winnall Moors nature reserve. The area hosts a collection of fens, meadows, chalk streams, reedbeds and wet woodlands rich in wetland species.

Winnall's wildlife includes significant populations of otters and water voles, as well as breeding Cetti's warbler. The Desmoulin's whorl snail inhabits the longer riverbank vegetation, and the hay meadows have a magnificent display of southern marsh orchids. These meadows were possibly the last known site in the Itchen Valley for breeding waders, such as snipe and redshank, before their eventual demise in the 1990s. Beneath the surface, the much feted wild brown trout feeds on the wealth of aquatic invertebrates including several species of mayfly and damselfly.

Over recent years the explosive song of the Cetti's warbler has been heard in increasing numbers through our river wetlands. © Dennis Bright

The streams and historic carriers that flow through Winnall Moors are classic chalk stream habitats and are an important historic fly fishery. River restoration work by the Trust in 2009 has increased the naturalness of the Barton carrier, benefiting wildlife and the fishery.
© Martin De Retuerto

In early summer the air above the streams at Winnall Moors can be thick with banded demoiselles.
© Ben Rushbrook

Thanks to donations from Trust members and grants, the Trust's ownership at Winnall Moors was nearly doubled in 2006; it is now undergoing a transformation through a major restoration project. The public area to the south has been made more attractive and accessible to visitors, who can now easily walk amongst reedbeds and fens. It is especially popular with workers who escape the office during their lunch break.

Further upstream the fen meadows are being restored and water levels raised to attract breeding snipe and redshank once again. Perhaps the most ambitious project is the re-naturalisation of the river itself. Following a long and sometimes rocky relationship with the fishing fraternity, the Trust is restoring diversity to the river to create more natural conditions and in tandem developing a more natural game fishery.

St Catherine's Hill nature reserve

The Trust's involvement with wildlife on the city limits of Winchester began in 1976 with a lease of St Catherine's Hill, which is owned by Winchester College, one of England's oldest schools. The Hill rises above the city and gives views across the Itchen Valley to the medieval grandeur of the Cathedral and the Hospital of St Cross. There is evidence of people living in and around St Catherine's Hill for over 3,000 years. The high ground of the Hill is readily defendable and so is crowned by the ramparts of a great fortress built some four hundred years before the arrival of the Romans. Within that fort are earthworks from the much earlier Bronze Age as well as the more recent Christian remains of a chapel dedicated to St Catherine.

Near the site of St Catherine's Chapel is a shape cut out of the turf, known as 'the mizmaze'. Mizmazes, first described in classical literature, are traditionally long winding paths along which the pilgrim walks to seek salvation. The St Catherine's Hill mizmaze appears to be of a more recent origin, a mere two hundred years or so. By repute the maze was cut by a schoolboy from Winchester College, although whether his inspiration was pagan, religious or a romantic allusion to classical times is unknown.

St Catherine's Hill is recognised as a Site of Special Scientific Interest for its rich chalk downland flora. The thin chalky soils of the slopes and summit are carpeted in closely-cropped sheep's fescue grassland, adorned with herbs including thyme, rock-rose, salad burnet and clustered bellflower.

Opposite: St Catherine's Hill rises out of the Itchen Valley above the historic city of Winchester.
© Albert Roberts

Clustered bellflower.
© Clive Chatters

The mizmaze. © Mark Heighes

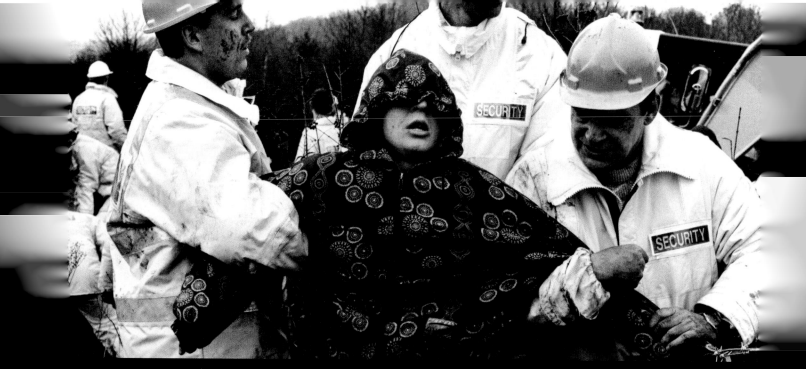

The Twyford Down debacle

One of the most controversial conservation battles in recent times involved the Trust and huge numbers of protestors. In the late 1980s it was proposed to route the M3 motorway through the Itchen Valley between St Catherine's Hill and the city of Winchester. The scheme was found to be unacceptable for its impact on the historic city and its meadow setting. A revised route, cutting through St Catherine's Hill, quickly followed and was strongly promoted by the government as part of its 'Roads for Prosperity' policy.

The protests against the scheme were vigorous and diverse. The Trust joined forces with the citizens of Winchester, eco-warriors and a variety of organisations to challenge the folly. From 1990 there was a cat-and-mouse campaign of protestors and security guards occupying and defending the construction site. On the 9th December 1992 a particularly belligerent eviction came to be known as 'Yellow Wednesday' after the fluorescent jackets of the guards.

Sadly, the protests ultimately failed to stop the works. By 1994 the road was being built. St Catherine's Hill is now divorced from the rest of the South Downs by an ugly cutting, a great gash through the Hill, through which the motorway now passes.

The latest twist to the story came in 2000. An experimental chalk grassland had been created to 'compensate' for the destruction of the slice of the nature reserve by the road. A new green sward was established to restore the route of the 1930s Winchester bypass so that it might once again be part of St Catherine's Hill. Without any apparent sense of shame it was duly announced that this land was now to be turned into a car park, appropriately to be called 'St Catherine's'.

Above and right: In the early 1990s the protest at Twyford Down drew nationwide attention to the government's road building policy. © Alex MacNaughton

Noar Hill nature reserve

Below: Noar Hill lies at the western end of the South Downs close to Selborne. A site of medieval chalk workings, the excavations left an irregular network of pits and hollows. It is now one of the last remaining fragments of ancient chalk downland in the area. Carpeted with wild flowers, the uneven terrain provides niches for a rich variety of species. Noar Hill has been managed by the Trust since the 1970s and is especially notable for its orchids and butterflies.
© Jon Oakley

Right: Noar Hill holds a nationally important population of the Duke of Burgundy fritillary. These beauties depend on lightly grazed downland with plenty of cowslips, and seem to prefer the more sheltered hollows.
© Graham Hoggarth

Bottom right: The caterpillar of the small blue butterfly feeds on kidney vetch which is an early colonist of disturbed nutrient-poor soils. This tiny, dusky blue butterfly is occasionally seen at Noar Hill.
© Ian Ralphs

115

THE HEATHS OF NORTH AND EAST HAMPSHIRE

UNTIL WELL INTO THE nineteenth century, the landscapes and rural life of north and east Hampshire were similar to today's New Forest. The mediaeval royal forest of Wolmer (now called Woolmer), together with the fragments of the once-vast Saxon forests of Windsor, Bagshot, Pamber and Eversley, had left a legacy of extensive heathland commons with scattered communities of graziers in farmsteads and small-holdings. Today these heaths are internationally important wildlife sites, protected under European law and known as the Thames Basin Heaths in the north and the Wealden Heaths in the east of the county.

On a warm summer's day the heaths burst with colour and interest. A walk across the heaths feeds the senses with the deep purple hues of heather, the bright yellow of gorse with its fabulous coconut scent, the flashes of green and blue from dragonflies, butterflies and tiger beetles, and the chance to see rare lizards and snakes.

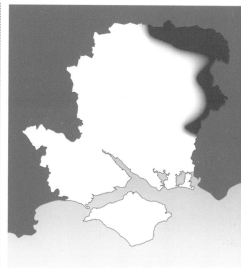

Opposite: A view of Caesar's Camp at Bricksbury Hill near Fleet. This scene will have remained relatively unchanged since the hill fort was built during the Iron Age, thanks to its continued use as a military training area.
© Alex Cruickshank

Gorse blooms throughout the year, with a peak in early summer. "When gorse is in flower, kissing's in season". © David Kilbey

Smooth snake. © Miha Krofel

Natterjack toad. © Daniel Kane

The Wealden Heaths of east Hampshire are the only place in Britain where all 12 species of our native reptile and amphibian can be found living together. Smooth snakes can be seen basking in open sandy patches, warming up in the early morning before moving off to feast on insects.

Woolmer is particularly important for the natterjack toad, a specialist of open sandy habitats and shallow temporary ponds. The natterjack's squat appearance, warty skin and distinctive yellow stripe are unmistakable.

Woolmer's acidic valley mires are important for *Sphagnum* mosses and other specialist plants such as round-leaved sundew, bog asphodel and white-beaked sedge.

Round-leaved sundew traps insects with sticky globules and digests them to gain a source of nitrogen, which is otherwise difficult to obtain in the water-logged conditions.

Bogs and heathland pools
fill low-lying hollows at Woolmer.
© Elliott Fairs

Round-leaved sundew.
© Alex Cruickshank

The wetlands of Woolmer are the only place in Britain where the spangled diving beetle can be found. This beetle lives up to its name with its gold and shimmering wing cases. It is found in several pools at Woolmer. Its preferred breeding area is Cranmer Pond, with adults emerging at the end of June.
© Dr Roger Key

The downy emerald is an eye-catching metallic green dragonfly with noticeable bright apple green eyes. It gains a bronze tinge with age, giving the adult a metallic sheen.
© Sebastian Dechert

The Thames Basin and Wealden Heaths are probably most famous for the three birds which give them their international conservation status. Dartford warbler, woodlark and nightjar are all rarities and highly protected.

On a warm summer evening, the gentle 'churring' of the nightjar is a magical sound, and the evidence that this well-camouflaged species is present. Looking remarkably like a pile of dead leaves, nightjars nest on the ground and can sometimes be seen chasing insects through dusky skies.

Nightjar. © Daniel Koh

A brief history of the heaths

The famous naturalist, the Reverend Gilbert White of Selborne, recorded the Wealden heaths and way of life in the latter half of the eighteenth century. *"The royal forest of Wolmer is a tract of land about seven miles in length, by two and a half in breadth.….The royalty consists entirely of sand covered with heath and fern; but is somewhat diversified with hills and dales, without having a standing tree in the whole extent. In the bottoms, where the water stagnates, are many bogs…."*

As well as observing the natural history of Selborne, Gilbert White was interested in its rural economy. He described how the heaths of Woolmer provided local people (commoners) with heathland turves and bog peat to provide fuel not only for their home fires but also for burning lime for their fields. The ashes of these fires were then used as a fertiliser for the grasslands. The heaths provided grazing for geese and cattle, in most part at little or no expense to the owners. Traditional rights of common secured the free use of the common by the villagers.

Not everyone was enamoured by the heath or the independence that commoners gained from their ancient rights. In 1810 Charles Vancouver of the Board of Agriculture referred to these open spaces as *"barren and dreary tracts"* and a *"nest and conservatory of sloth, idleness and misery"*. His recommendations to the government were for the complete destruction of commons and forests. In 1812 Parliament passed a Deforestation Act affecting 5,242 acres of Woolmer alone.

The Enclosure movement all but killed off the commoning way of life. In 1811 over 1,200 acres of heathland commons were enclosed at Farnborough. In 1856 over 660 acres were enclosed at Liss with an additional 1,100 acres of the adjacent Woolmer Forest enclosed two years later. In most cases the enclosed heathland commons were taken into the growing towns or converted into forestry plantations. The better soils were farmed but these were still hungry lands that needed considerable investment to make them profitable. By the 1850s the railways had been established across Hampshire and with them came an increasingly industrial and urban economy. Towns grew up along the railway, the economy was changing, agriculture and subsistence farming were being displaced by manufacturing and the many opportunities of urban life. The heathlands of north and east Hampshire today are the last relics of this once great open landscape.

The small red damselfly is a nationally scarce species that is restricted to heathland sites in southern England and in Wales. At Woolmer, it is often seen hovering a few centimeters above shallow boggy pools.
© Mark Heighes

A view across Woolmer from Queen's Bank.
© Alex Cruickshank

The Trust, the Army and the heaths

The survival of the largest heathlands is due to their appropriation for military training in the nineteenth century. The British Army, which has its home at Aldershot, needed local training grounds for exercises including gunnery practice and cavalry training. Today the Army uses the heaths for vehicle testing and manoeuvres, and as a small arms range. The heaths have been kept free from intensive farming, forestry and urban development to permit the army to train.

The 9 (Parachute) Squadron Royal Engineers train at Long Valley near their base in Aldershot, in preparation for deployment to Afghanistan, January 2002.
© Imperial War Museum, HU 99486

In June 1962, the Trust's Conservation Committee expressed *"concern as for the uncared for condition of many heaths and commons owned or managed by the War Dept."* Later that year it was agreed that the Trust *"should furnish a report which will be submitted to the Command Land Agent in an attempt to obtain the Army's co-operation. Places of special importance are Fleet Pond, Woolmer Pond, Woolmer Ranges, Bourley, Long Valley, Weavers Down. It was emphasised that a measure of scrub clearance is essential."*

Through the spring and summer of 1963, there were discussions between the Trust and the Army, resulting in the establishment of a conservation committee for the Longmoor Camp on the Woolmer Ranges. The Trust asked Lady Anne Brewis to attend on its behalf. Lady Anne was the daughter of the 3rd Earl of Selborne, a zoologist by training and a botanist by passion. For nearly 30 years the committee benefited from her expert and forthright contributions. By 1974 this local initiative had grown into the Longmoor Conservation Group, the first of 160 such groups now covering Ministry of Defence sites across Britain and abroad.

It was through these meetings that the wildlife of the military lands was explored and celebrated. Specialist groups were encouraged to undertake surveys and modest conservation projects. The scale of the task was awesome. There are 2,900 hectares of heathland within the military estate in Hampshire; a few weekends of scrub clearance by volunteers was clearly not going to be sufficient.

During the 1980s and 90s the needs of the Army were changing, with a need for more open habitats rather than forests. At the same time there was increased political momentum for wildlife conservation, following the 1992 Rio Earth Summit. Now the UK Government's commitments were in tune with the Trust's long-held desire to see the heaths restored.

At this time the fundamental importance of grazing in heathland ecosystems was becoming better understood. Grazing not only holds back the rough grasses and scrub that can colonise heathlands, but also improves the habitat of specialist species by the physical processes of grazing, including the scuffing of hooves and the redistribution of nutrients through dung and urine. Modern ecological science was confirming the observations of Gilbert White from an earlier century. If the heathlands were to be restored it would be necessary to re-instate grazing.

The common butterwort is confined to a handful of sites in lowland heaths and fens. The restoration of grazing at Eelmoor Marsh provided abundant broken ground which was rapidly colonised by both the pale and common butterworts.
© Jón Ágúst Guðjónsson

Bringing back grazing

The first big step in making a difference came in 1995, when the Defence Research Agency (now QinetiQ) adjacent to Farnborough Airfield introduced livestock to the heaths and wetlands of Eelmoor Marsh. The high-security fencing around this fragment of Cove Common assisted grazing to be established, in this case led by Marwell Preservation Trust (now Marwell Wildlife) with a bachelor herd of endangered Przewalski's horses. The results were spectacular, as rare plants such as marsh helleborine and butterwort started to reappear, and a wave of enthusiasm spread out from Eelmoor Marsh to the rest of the Defence Estate.

It was not long after the successes of Eelmoor Marsh that the Army approached the Trust to discuss estate management. Following understandably complex negotiations, in 2004 the Trust took on obligations to work with the Army to restore over 2,000 hectares of their heaths, stretching from Minley through Aldershot and down to Longmoor.

The initial challenge for this new project was the landscape-scale clearance of rank grassland, scrub and stands of alien conifers. The re-establishment of grazing required a massive investment in perimeter fences and stock handling facilities, as well as public relations. The design of the infrastructure needed not only to take account of military training needs and conservation management needs, but also the expectations of the public who enjoy access to the heaths.

Opposite: The silver-studded blue butterfly is abundant on our grazed heaths. The caterpillars feed on bird's-foot trefoil, heather and gorse and are tended by ants which feed on their sticky secretions.
© Ben Rushbrook

Possibly the greatest challenge of all was to find grazing animals that would do well on heathland pastures. In large parts of north Hampshire, agriculture has declined as the urban areas have grown. Farming enterprises with livestock around the northern heaths are few and far between. Enterprises with hardy stock suited to rough grazing are even rarer. It was an important decision by the Trust not to set up its own herd of animals but rather to work with local graziers, to build partnerships to support and expand their businesses. Such an approach aims to promote economic reasons for heathland grazing in addition to conservation.

By 2007 everything had come together and was celebrated with the release of 25 head of cattle onto the newly fenced Velmead Common. By 2010 there were nearly 200 cattle spread over six sites covering over 830 hectares of heath. There is still a great deal more to do, with plans for substantial additional areas of heath to be fenced and grazed over the next few years.

Stag's-horn clubmoss, a great rarity in Hampshire that is now booming on the north Hampshire heaths due to habitat recovery.
© Alex Cruickshank

The ancient traditions of heathland grazing are revived as cattle are returned to Velmead Common.
© Sarah Clark

The heathland landscapes and economy of today are different from those of Gilbert White's time, yet there are common elements. The heaths are being rejuvenated as great open landscapes rich in wildlife. The livestock that graze the heaths are no longer the mixed herds of many commoners exercising ancient rights. Today's livestock are supported for their ability to maintain the heaths, to revive local agricultural enterprises and to grow high quality local food. The greatest change is that the heaths are now seen as an important local amenity for a huge resident population. In the distant past these wild open spaces may have enthused, or appalled, the occasional wandering cleric or civil servant. Today they are the green lungs for the hundreds and thousands of people who live around their borders.

In the winter cattle graze on heather bushes and seedling trees.
© Alex Cruickshank

The woodlark is a ground-nesting bird which breeds on the heaths of north and east Hampshire. It is a conservation success story with numbers on the increase where suitable habitat has been restored. At its lowest point in 1986 there were just 241 breeding pairs in the UK but this has now risen to more than 3,000.
© Chris Gomershall (rspb-images.com)

Public access and conservation

In recent years the Trust has been increasingly engaged in debates with planners about the consequences of increased access to the Thames Basin Heaths. An estimated five million people use the heaths every year for informal recreation, principally dog walking. Studies conducted in Dorset have shown that regular disturbance from such use has a significant negative impact on the breeding success of woodlark, nightjar and Dartford warbler. The Trust has been working with other partners, in particular the RSPB, to promote solutions to the problem of increasing urban growth on the heathland fringes. The same challenges are facing the New Forest and the south Hampshire coastline. It is now being recognised that our heathlands and other vulnerable habitats must not be the only open spaces available to urban populations and that alternative accessible green spaces are needed.

Bartley Heath nature reserve

By the 1980s the tradition of grazing heathlands in north Hampshire had dwindled to a single common, Bartley Heath. Together with the adjacent village greens at North Warnborough, Bartley Heath was given to the Trust in 1987 in memory of Mr and Mrs Clegg, the founders of Ladybird Books. This superb area of ancient countryside had unfortunately been targeted by highway planners in the 1970s. The nature reserve is not only crossed by the M3 motorway but was also chosen to accommodate Junction 5. When the Trust received the gift, what was once a single site had been broken into ten fragments, separated from one another by busy roads. These fragments were in a sorry state with the exception of an area near Hook where the Champion family continued to exercise their ancient common grazing rights. The grazing of the common by the Champions' ponies and cattle, combined with scrub clearance by the Trust, is encouraging heathland beauties such as the marsh gentian to thrive.

Plants can be more resilient to such upheavals than some butterflies. Bartley Heath was one of the last places in north Hampshire where the marsh fritillary flew. Sadly it is now locally extinct. This is a butterfly of flower-rich heathland and grassland, the caterpillars feeding on devil's-bit scabious. Marsh fritillaries may only fly a hundred metres or so in their lifetime yet they need large landscapes to thrive. Over a number of years, parasites build up in populations of their caterpillars, and so fresh colonies need to be forming as others dwindle. The caterpillars need reasonably large plants of devil's-bit scabious, so continuous hard grazing is far from ideal; equally no grazing leads to the plants being swamped by rank grassland.

A Third Book of
BRITISH BIRDS
and their nests
A LADYBIRD NATURE BOOK

Opposite: A Highland cow, belonging to the local commoner, grazing on Bartley Heath.
© Laura Fairs

A Third Book of British Birds and their Nests by Brian Vesey-Fitzgerald, illustrated by Roland Green. © Ladybird Books Ltd, 1956. Reproduced by permission of Ladybird Books Ltd.

The devil's-bit scabious is a plant of damp habitats and inhabits marshes, moist meadows and wet woodland. It is the food plant of the marsh fritillary. It is said that its name may come from a legend that the devil bit off the roots of the plant, as he was envious of their ability to calm nerves.
Credit: © Chris Bean

Left: Marsh gentian is thriving at Bartley Heath following the restoration of grazing. © Elliott Fairs

Pamber Forest nature reserve

At the western limits of the Thames Basin Heaths, the soils become deeper and richer and heathland progressively gives way to woodland and fertile pastures.

Between the villages of Tadley and Silchester, not far from the Berkshire border, is a series of small heathland commons. A walk across Silchester Common takes you through a fringe of open woodland into a landscape of gentle undulations. Cattle roam freely across the common, resting in the shade of birch groves on hot summer days or wandering into the wet valley bottoms to enjoy the lusher grasslands. As they range through the common so they may find their way into the funnel-shaped lanes that penetrate the adjacent blocks of woodland. Here and there are open-grown oaks with the ancient trees along the woodland banks; elsewhere are sunny glades of heathers and grasses. The woodlands are bound by a network of earthworks, each section bearing its own name. This intertwining of wood and common is surrounded by a landscape of small fields with wildlife-rich hedgerows. In season, many of these fields are full of wildflowers, insects and birdsong. This intimate piece of countryside is a survivor of the historic Pamber Forest, itself a fragment of the ancient Forest of Windsor.

The woods of Pamber Forest were some of the first places in Hampshire to be recognised as of national importance for wildlife. In 1952 the woods were designated under recent legislation as a Site of Special Scientific Interest. These woodlands were exceptional as a place where traditional woodcrafts thrived, supporting management by coppicing. Sections of the woods were cut in rotation to produce small wood, bringing with it a cycle of sunshine and shade across the woodland floor. This is ideal habitat for the many species of our ancient woodlands, particularly moths and butterflies, which prefer sunlight and open ground to permanent woodland shade.

The delightfully named drab looper moth benefits from occasional clearance of trees as its caterpillars feed on wilted and withered oak leaves. To be suitable for the caterpillar, these leaves have to be in humid, but not too dark, woodland.
© Jon Oakley

The purple emperor flies high in the forest within the canopy of the oak trees. © Pete Eeles, Butterfly Conservation

Wild daffodils line the woodland streams of Pamber Forest.
© Charles Cuthbert

Wood spurge is a woodland plant tolerant of the dark conditions of a closed canopy. Even in the darkest woods, this spurge can thrive when other woodland flowers cannot. The ability to persist means that after coppicing wood spurge is already present and able to take immediate advantage of the extra light. These well illuminated plants are the food plant of the misnamed 'common' fan foot moth. The caterpillars of this nationally scarce moth are able to feed on the spurge, in spite of its acrid, poisonous sap.

Through the 1950s there was a decline in the local coppice industry upon which Pamber Forest's woodland wildlife depends. By the early 1960s the market for most coppice work had collapsed. A few craftsmen held on until recent years, making woodland products such as besom brooms, but this was small-scale work and not capable of maintaining a whole landscape. As the coppices grew up and were left uncut, so the wildlife that followed the woodsman's axe fell into decline.

The majority of the woodlands of Pamber Forest are owned by the Englefield Estate, a great country estate straddling the borders of Berkshire and Hampshire. In 1980 the Estate, in partnership with the local authority, declared Pamber Forest a Local Nature Reserve, to be managed for wildlife and public amenity. Prominent on the Pamber Forest Management Committee was the neighbourhood GP, Dr Peter Brough. Peter knew his local community and was well respected. Peter brought to the committee his expertise as a 'naturalist physician'. For many years he served on this group and was Chairman of the Wildlife Trust's Conservation Committee. He was also co-author of the 'Flora of Hampshire'.

Under Peter's guidance the management of the woodlands at Pamber Forest was restored. Reassurances were needed for people who loved the Forest, such as in 1986 when 750 mature oaks were felled to bring sunlight back into the shady rides. By the early 1990s coppicing was once again an important part of the woodland landscape. The response of butterflies was spectacular and the displays of woodland wildflowers were equally impressive.

Butterfly species such as this white admiral have responded dramatically to the re-instatement of coppicing at Pamber Forest, which now holds some of the strongest populations in Hampshire. © Jon Oakley

The mixture of woodland types mean that Pamber Forest is one of the richest places in southern England for 'ancient woodland indicator' plant species, which tend to be confined to wooded habitats of great antiquity and have a poor ability to colonise new woodlands. Pamber Forest has 66 of these species including Solomon's seal (left), lily-of-the-valley, wild daffodil and wild service tree. © David Ellison

In the late 1990s the Trust took on the direct responsibility for the management of the Forest as a nature reserve. At over 200 hectares, Pamber Forest is one of the Trust's largest reserves. The majority of the Forest remains in the ownership of the Estate, yet there are also islands of woodland owned by local farmers. Most, but not all, of the heathland is owned by the Parish Council. In 2001 the Trust was able to buy Inhams Copse, in the valley on the eastern side of Pamber Forest, following a bequest by Gwen Talmay. Here is a landscape where wildlife is unconstrained by artificial borders, and the cattle, visitors and butterflies move freely across the boundaries of ownership.

The fly agaric toadstool grows in the woodland edge grasslands of Pamber Forest.
© Alex Cruickshank

Ron Ward's Meadow nature reserve

On a gentle hillside to the west of Pamber is a brick and flint tomb. This marks the grave of Ron Ward, a local man with deep roots in the countryside and a love of nature. In the summer of 1991 the hillside was made a Site of Special Scientific Interest in recognition of it being an exceptionally rich wildflower grassland; the official name given to the designation was 'Ron Ward's Meadow'. A few weeks later Ron died. His body was carried through the village to the tomb that he had built for himself overlooking his beloved meadow. Ron's final wish was for his meadow to be made a nature reserve and so he gifted the land to the Trust. Each year as the meadow comes to bloom it does so overseen by Ron's tomb, a timely reminder of how much of the wildlife and wild places of our two counties we owe to the passion of local people.

Ron Ward's Meadow.
© Jon Oakley

THE LONG VIEW

FIFTY YEARS IS A SPECK in time. The last half century has been an incredibly important period in the history of our land and sea. The scale and pace of change in the natural environment has had profound effects that we ignore at our peril. Fifty years has been long enough for the Trust to start to make a difference, yet the job is far from complete.

The rate of destruction of our largest and richest wildlife habitats has been slowed. Yet what is left is a fraction of what once existed. Many threats remain, and some are becoming ever more pressing. On a global scale, climate change is now accepted and discussed amongst world leaders. On a more local level, securing our food, water, fibre and fuel is placing ever greater demands on the countryside. The urban growth planned for our two counties runs to many tens of thousands of houses. The demands of leisure and access to fresh air and open space need also to be accommodated. The competition for the use of both land and sea is intense. As wild nature cannot speak for itself, it is up to the Trust to ensure it is not overlooked.

The government development agency for south-east England has recently published research into the unsustainable nature of our way of life. South-east England is the most economically buoyant region in England yet this is being achieved at an unacceptable cost. A measure of that lack of sustainability is a growing loss of the quality of our environment, and the quality of our lives.

Wild nature cannot function in a series of small, isolated fragments of habitat. The 'intensive care' management of a nature reserve may provide a fighting chance for some species, but in the long run they are vulnerable to the world changing around them. The future for wildlife will depend upon the success of a joined up approach to managing our landscape and economy. It will also depend upon people starting to adopt a more sustainable way of life, one where nature is truly valued. The Trust's work is now reaching out far beyond the individual splendours of nature reserves, to find common ground with neighbours and with anyone else whose decisions affect wildlife and wild places.

Opposite: Looking from Oxey Marsh across to Yarmouth on the Isle of Wight.
© Linda Priestley

Nature reserves will continue to be a central aspect of the Trust's approach to nature conservation. Not only will the Trust's reserves include inspirationally rich places, but also places with a practical purpose. Each meadow, heath or down needs an adjacent area to care for the livestock that graze it. Each coppice needs space where the crop of small wood can be stored and worked up to enhance its value. The Trust recognises the importance of supporting rural enterprises that in turn maintain the right conditions for nature. A strong livestock sector, providing animals for grazing, will benefit wildlife far beyond the borders of our landholdings, as will a good market for small wood products. Similarly, genuinely sustainable fisheries, marine industry and leisure will secure the future of marine life together with the livelihoods of those who depend upon the sea.

Given the scale of the challenge to protect our wildlife and wild places, the Trust is fortunately not alone in its work. The Hampshire & Isle of Wight Trust combines with the 46 other Wildlife Trusts across the UK to influence national government policy. The Trust is also positive about working with national organisations with which we share common goals, including bodies such as the RSPB and the National Trust.

Half of the world's population of the grey seal is found in British waters, and numbers have doubled since the 1960s. Grey seals are regular visitors to our local seas, travelling from their breeding grounds in south-west England and the southern North Sea.
© Matt Doggett

Opposite: Birdwatching at Swanwick Lakes, one of the Trust's nature reserves and education centres.
© Peter Hutchings

Hampshire & Isle of Wight Wildlife Trust is a strong, influential and well-supported local nature conservation charity. Membership of the Trust has grown from 79 members in 1961, to 1,000 members in 1965, 10,000 in 1995 and today stands at over 28,000. This impressive membership not only gives the Trust financial security, but it is recognised and respected by decision makers, adding extra weight and credence to the Trust's arguments.

Fifty years ago, the founders of the Trust recognised challenges that are still relevant today. The Trust must continue to act as a champion for wildlife and wild places in debates on planning and development. It must help those in power to understand the importance of the environment when making their decisions.

The Trust also needs to help upcoming generations understand their role in securing the quality of the world in which they, and their children, will live. The Trust fundamentally believes that everyone has the right to a quality of life in which wild nature plays its part, enriching people's lives. The Trust's challenge is to inspire and enthuse the next generation in an increasingly urbanised world.

Above all the Trust is *the* local, passionate, approachable, knowledgeable and resolute champion for our wildlife heritage. The Trust represents continuity of purpose and an unwavering determination to be the voice for nature in our two counties. The Trust is proud of the achievements of its first 50 years and looks forward to turning the tide in favour of nature in the future.

Hampshire & Isle of Wight
Wildlife Trust

Protecting wildlife. Inspiring people.

THE
wildlife
TRUSTS